the starving artist...

the eyes that feel, the hands that see

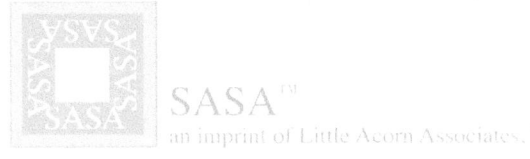

SASA™
an imprint of Little Acorn Associates, Inc.

the starving artist...
the eyes that feel, the hands that see

©2012 SASA™

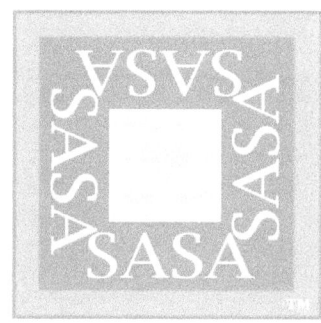

SASA™ is an imprint of little acorn associates, inc.

published by
little acorn associates, inc.
all rights reserved.

publication number: SASA-1212
ISBN 978-1-937257-15-6

all image copyrights remain with each individual artist

no portion or portions of this publication may be copied or reproduced in any format
whatsoever without verified written permission from the publisher.

the starving artist...
the eyes that feel, the hands that see

dedicated to all who create

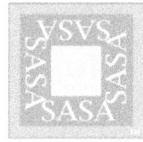

contents

the eyes that feel, the hands that see—........ 1
barr, m g... 3
campbell-thomas, barbara....................... 4
ananian, michael............................... 8
barr, m g... 13
barr, j a... 14
mckenzie, alex................................. 17
morris, christopher h.......................... 22
pintado, steisha............................... 26
said, ibrahim.................................. 30
stephan, mariam................................ 34
barr, m g... 38
moore, maurice................................. 40
tisdell, suzanne............................... 43
robinson, miranda.............................. 47
shipman, bennett............................... 50
belluardo, s a................................. 56
barr, m g... 57
swift, nicholas................................ 58
neff, j... 63
richardson, herbert............................ 68
godden, anna................................... 71
foust, s....................................... 74
rivera, graciela............................... 76
barr, m g... 78
alphabetical listing of
    the eyes that feel,the hands that see....... 80

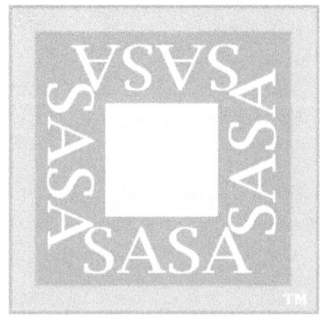

the eyes that feel, the hands that see

the eyes that feel, the hands that see
cannot be
empty vessels,
vacuums,
dormant,
exiled,
deprived,
abused,
inert,
barren,
hollow,
isolated,
discharged,
vacant,
unused,
suppressed,
desolate,
depleted,
void,
malnourished,
hungry,
starving—

lest prolonged starvation cause permanent damage,
and death of the visually charged—
    the painter, the sculptor, the designer,
    the photographer, the engraver, the illustrator,
    the artist, the maker,
    the eyes that feel, the hands that see—
ensues

barr, m g

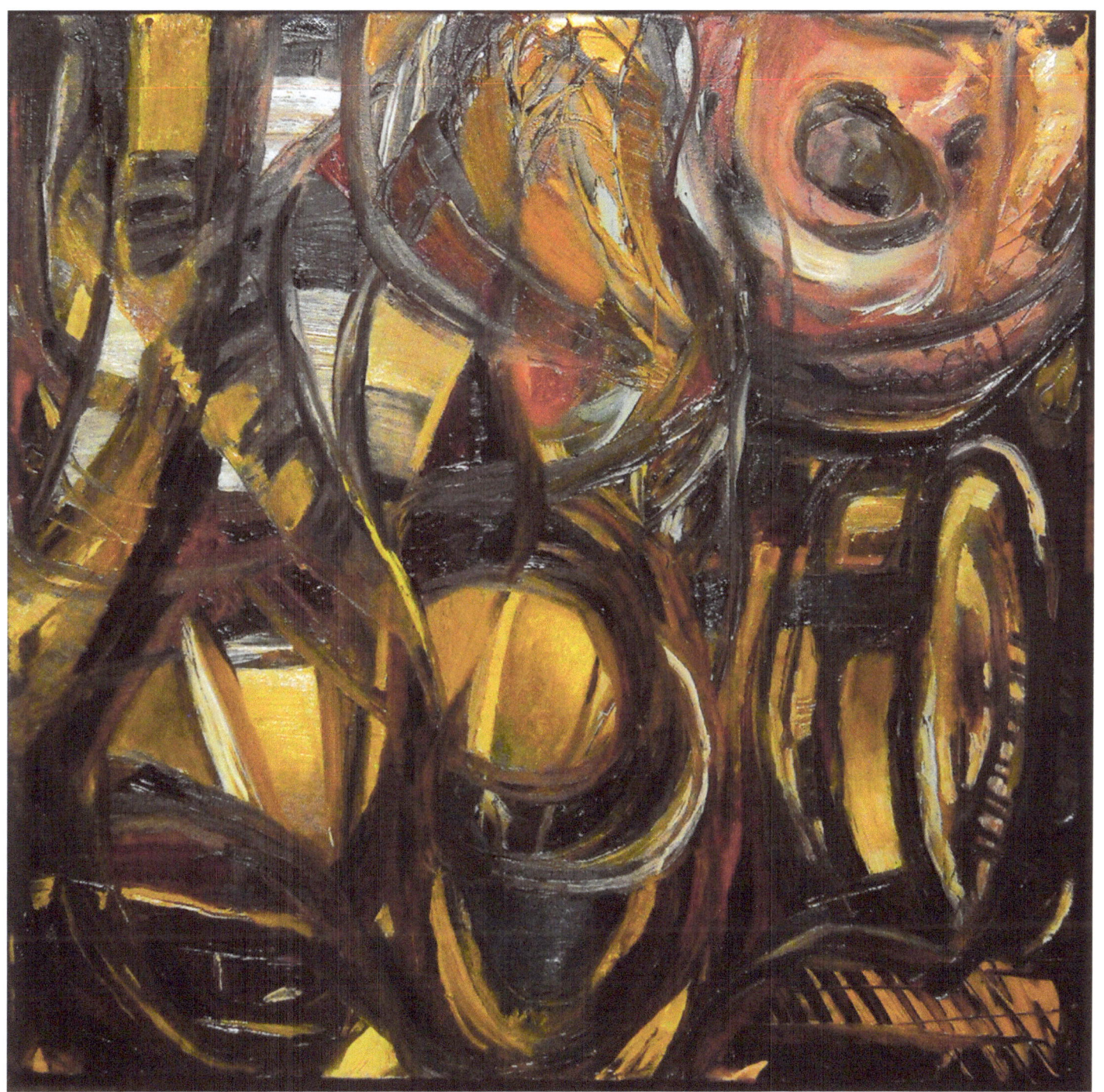

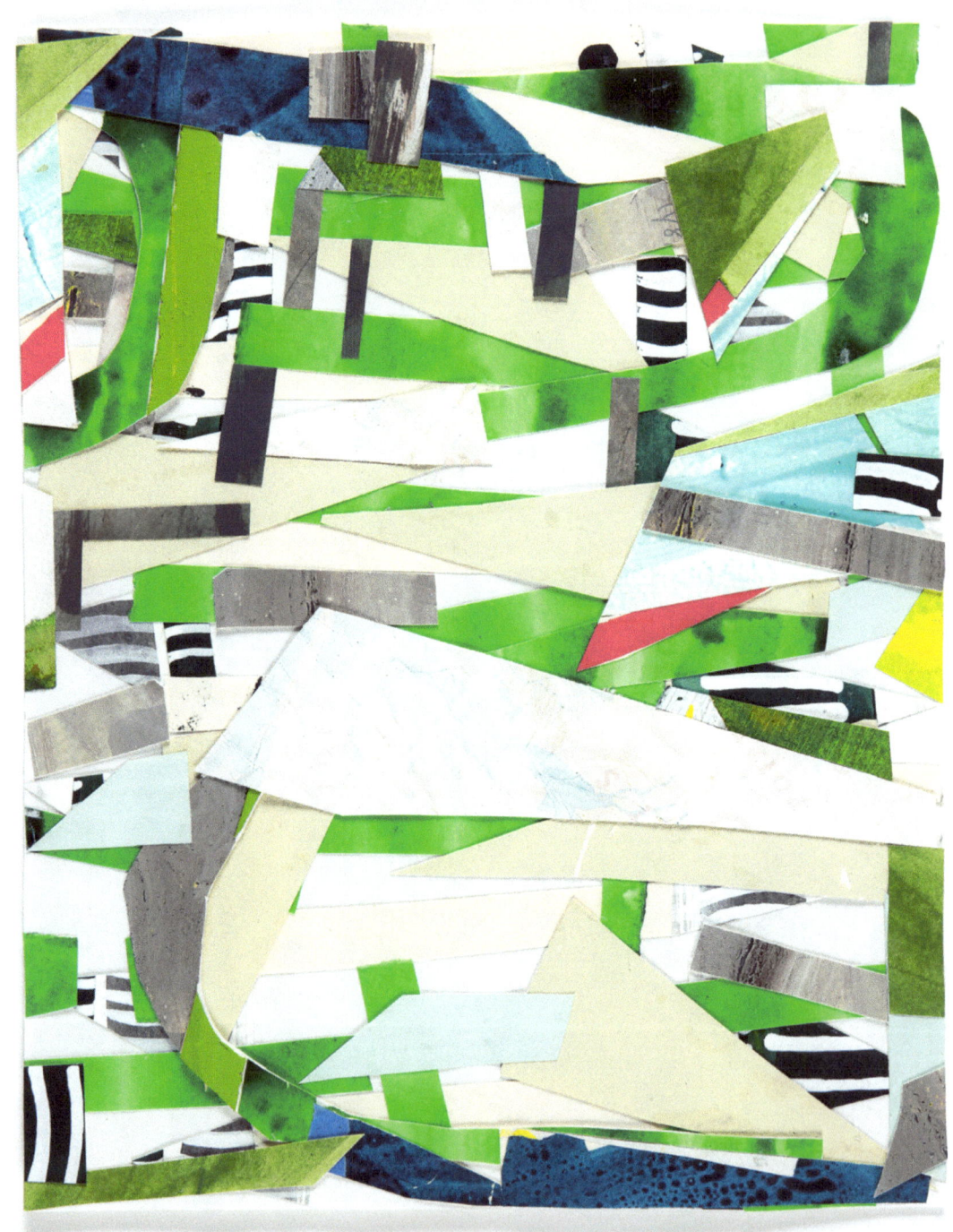

campbell-thomas, barbara

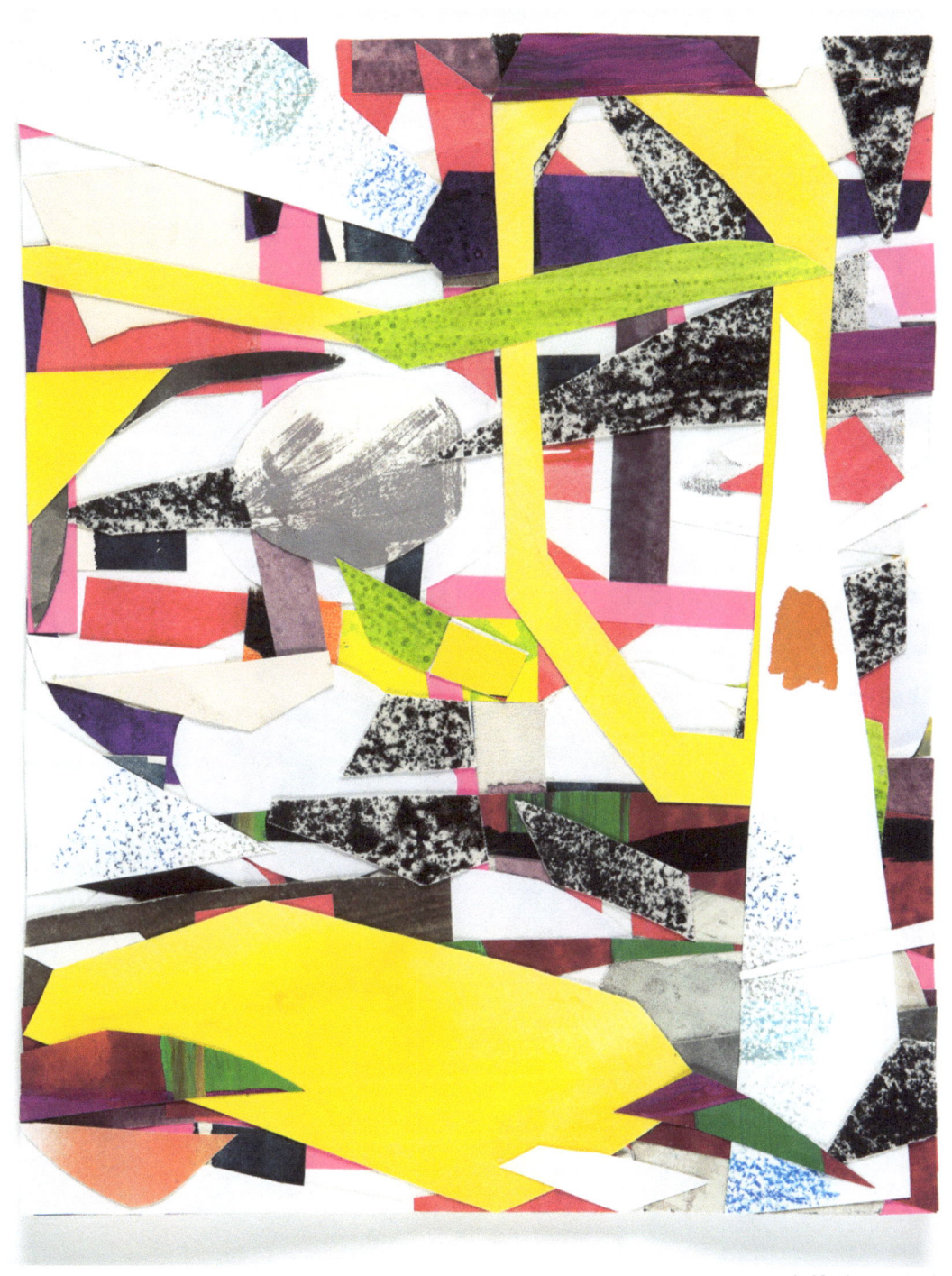

campbell-thomas, barbara

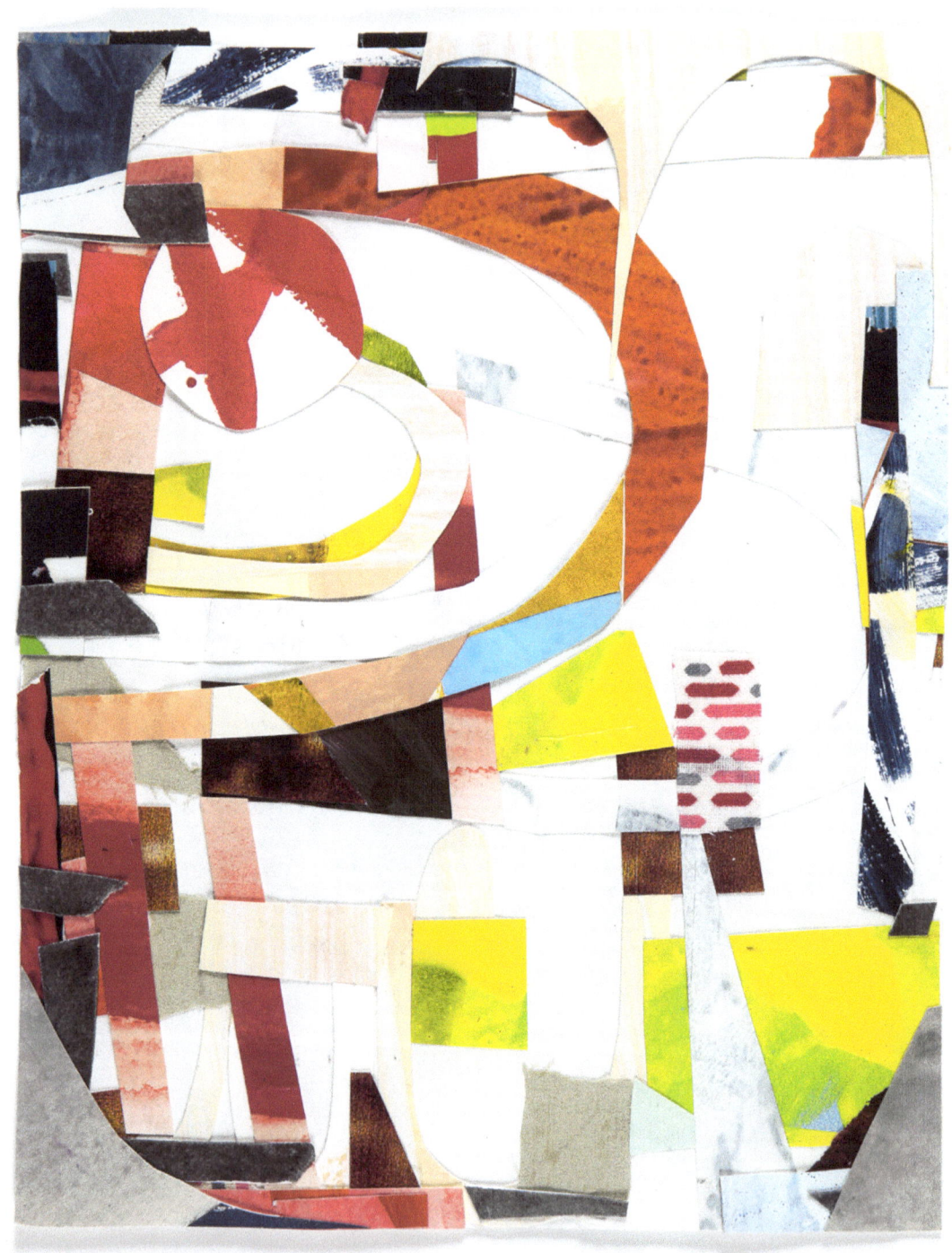

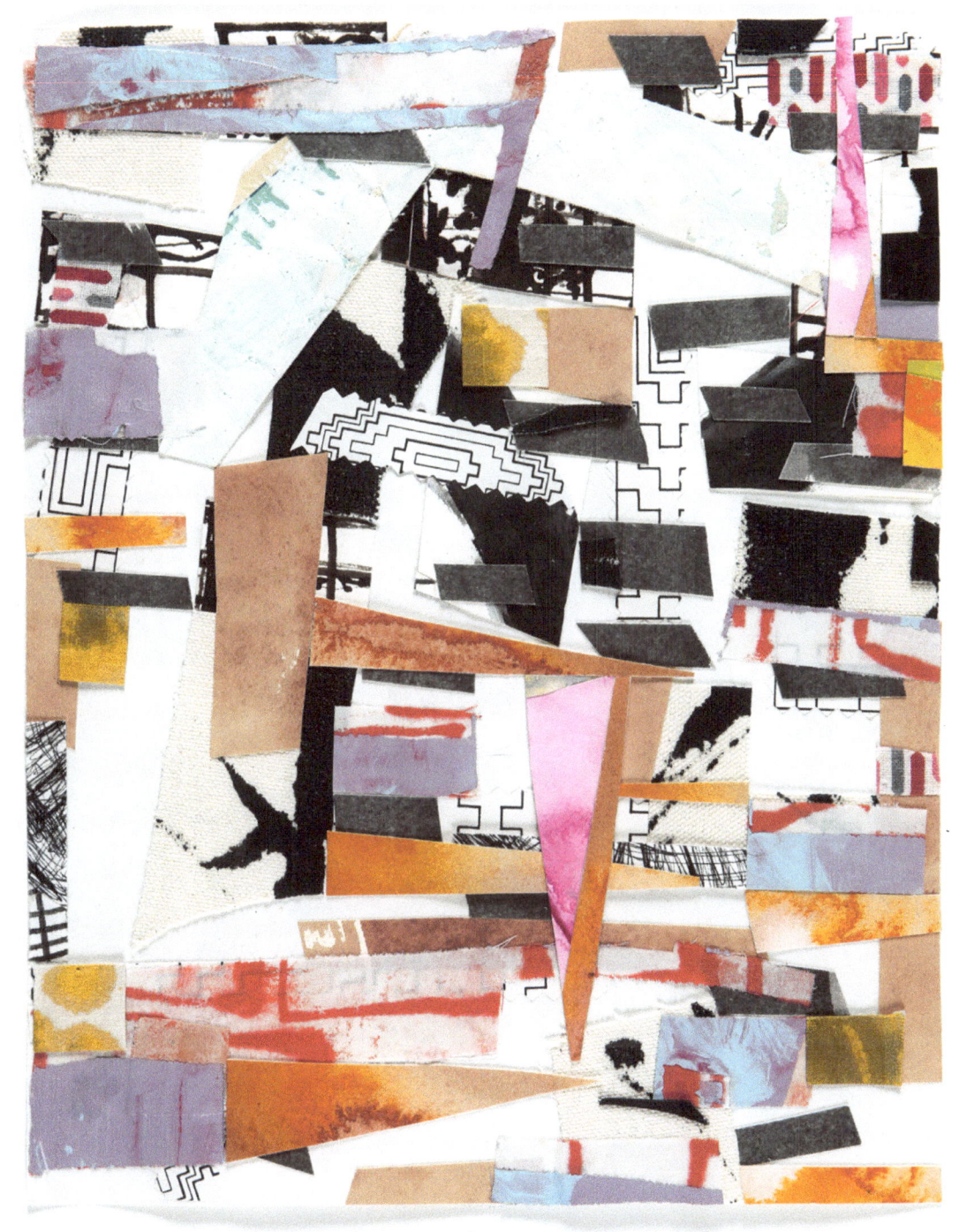

campbell-thomas, barbara

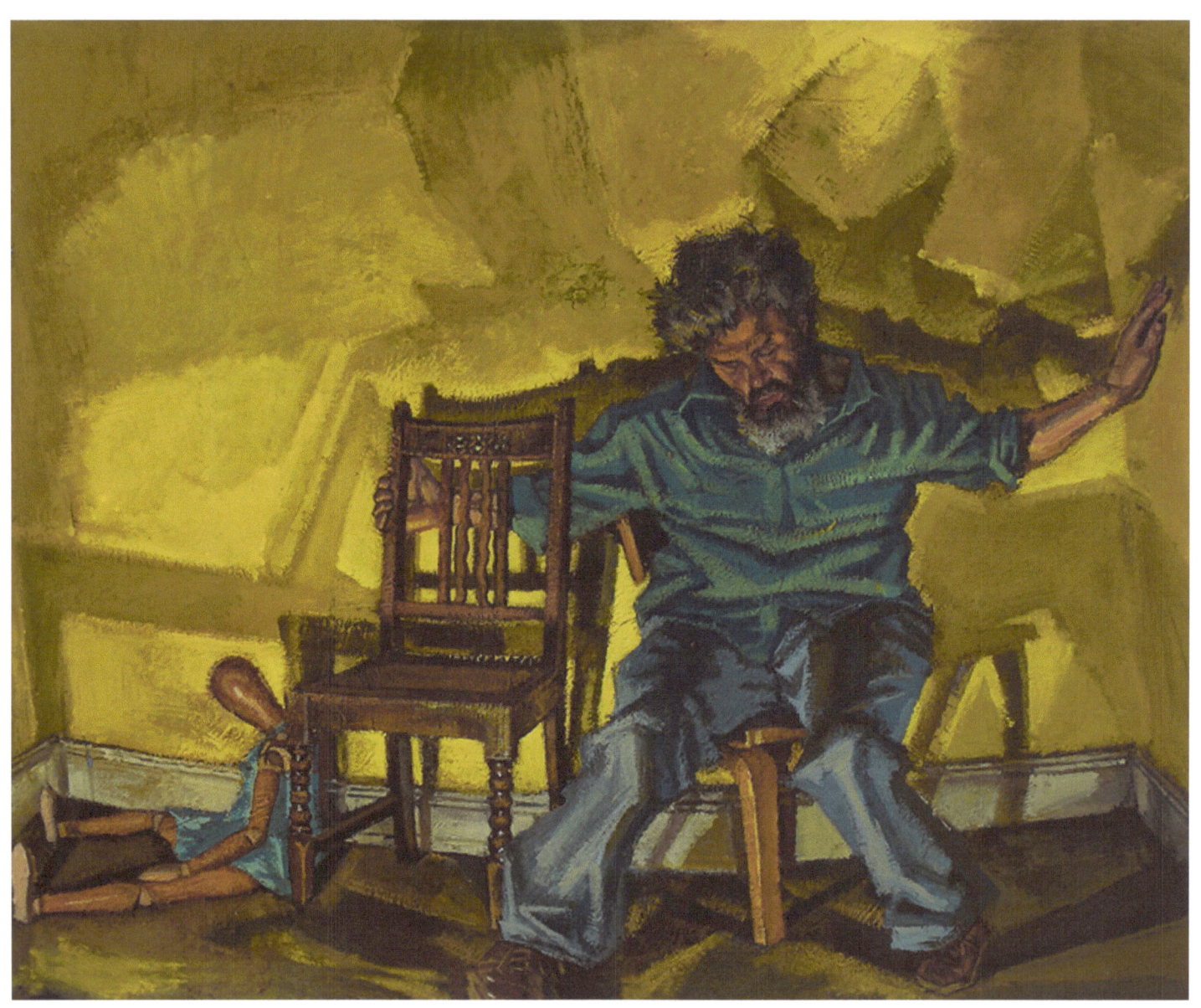

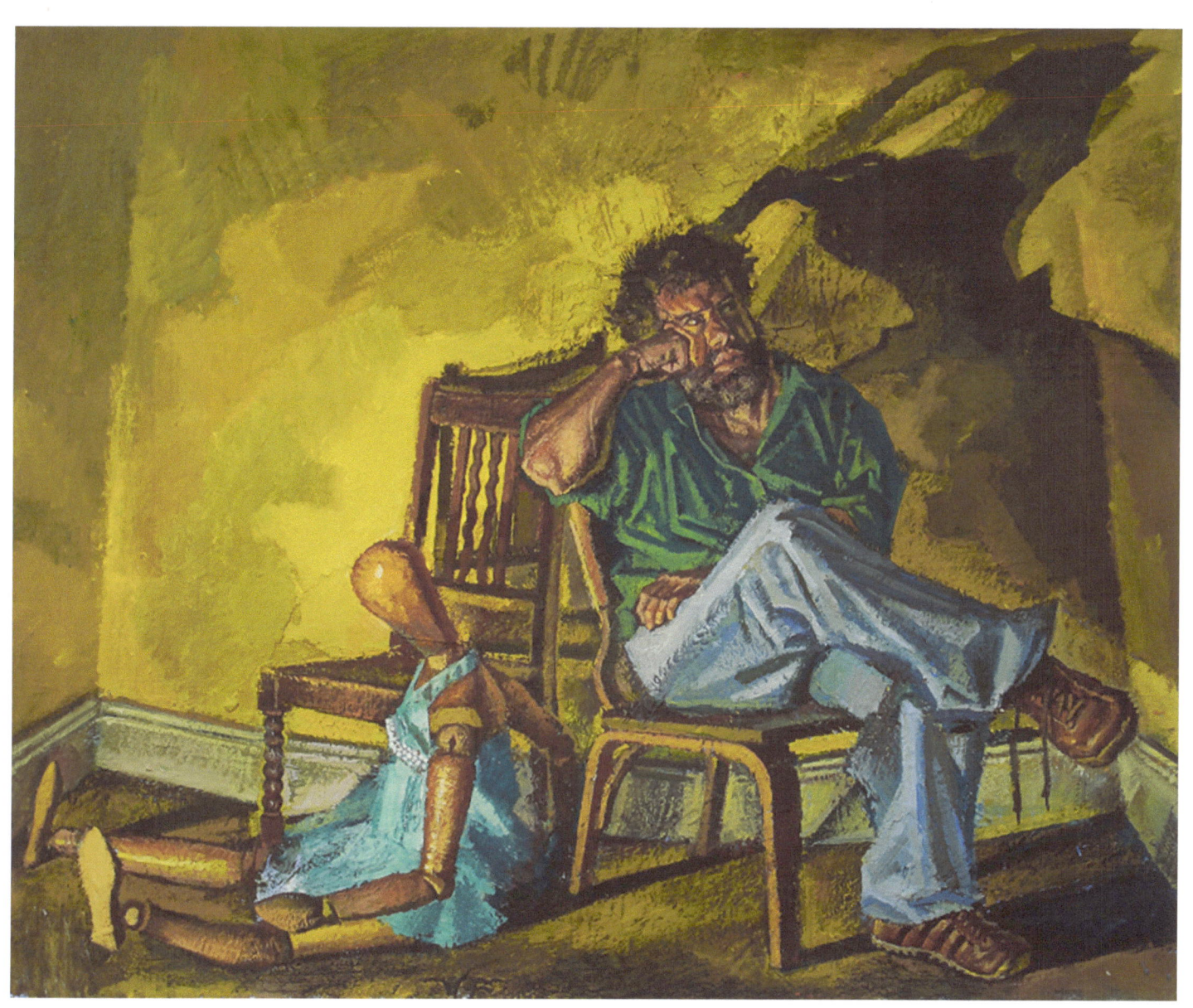

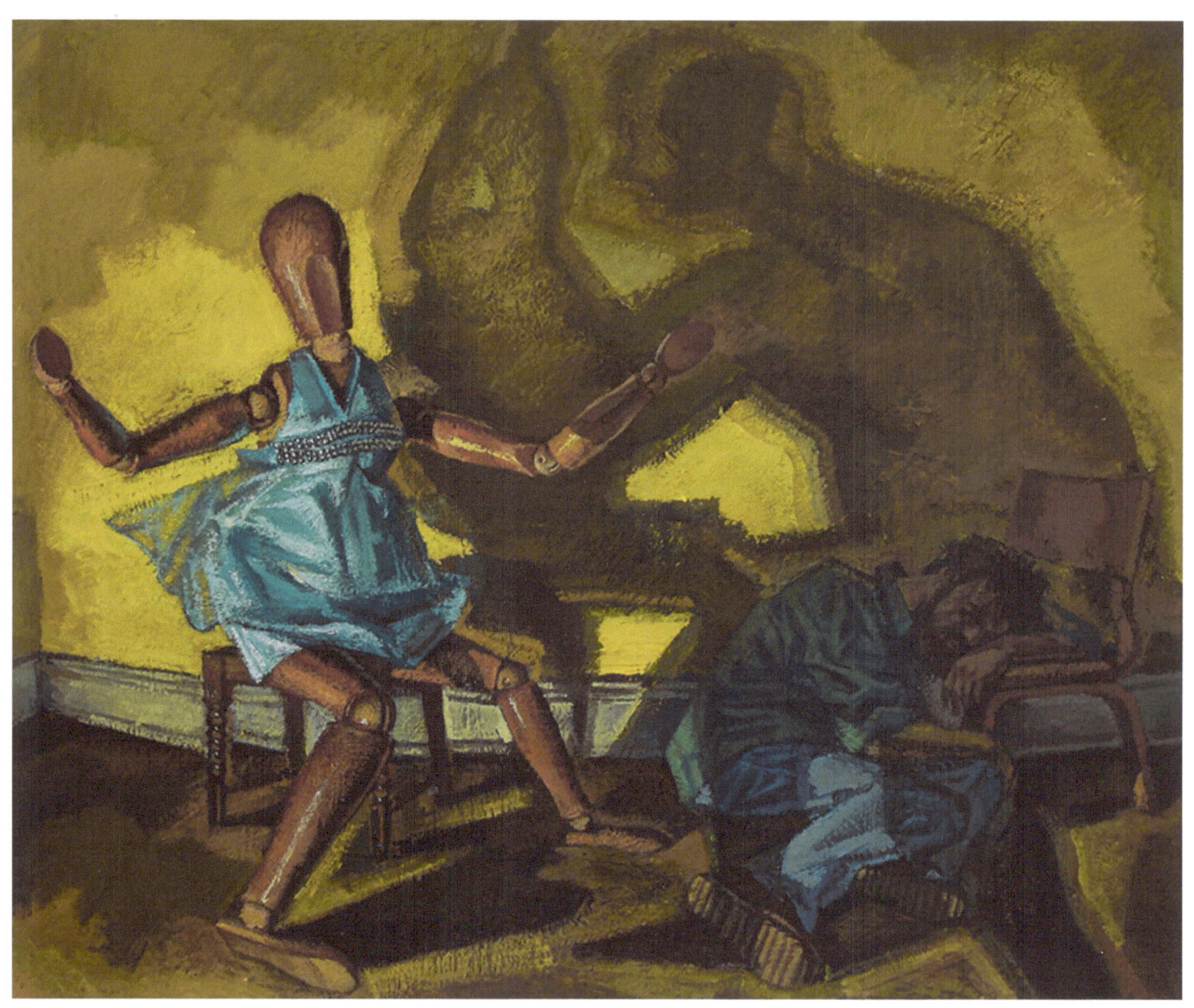

ananian, michael

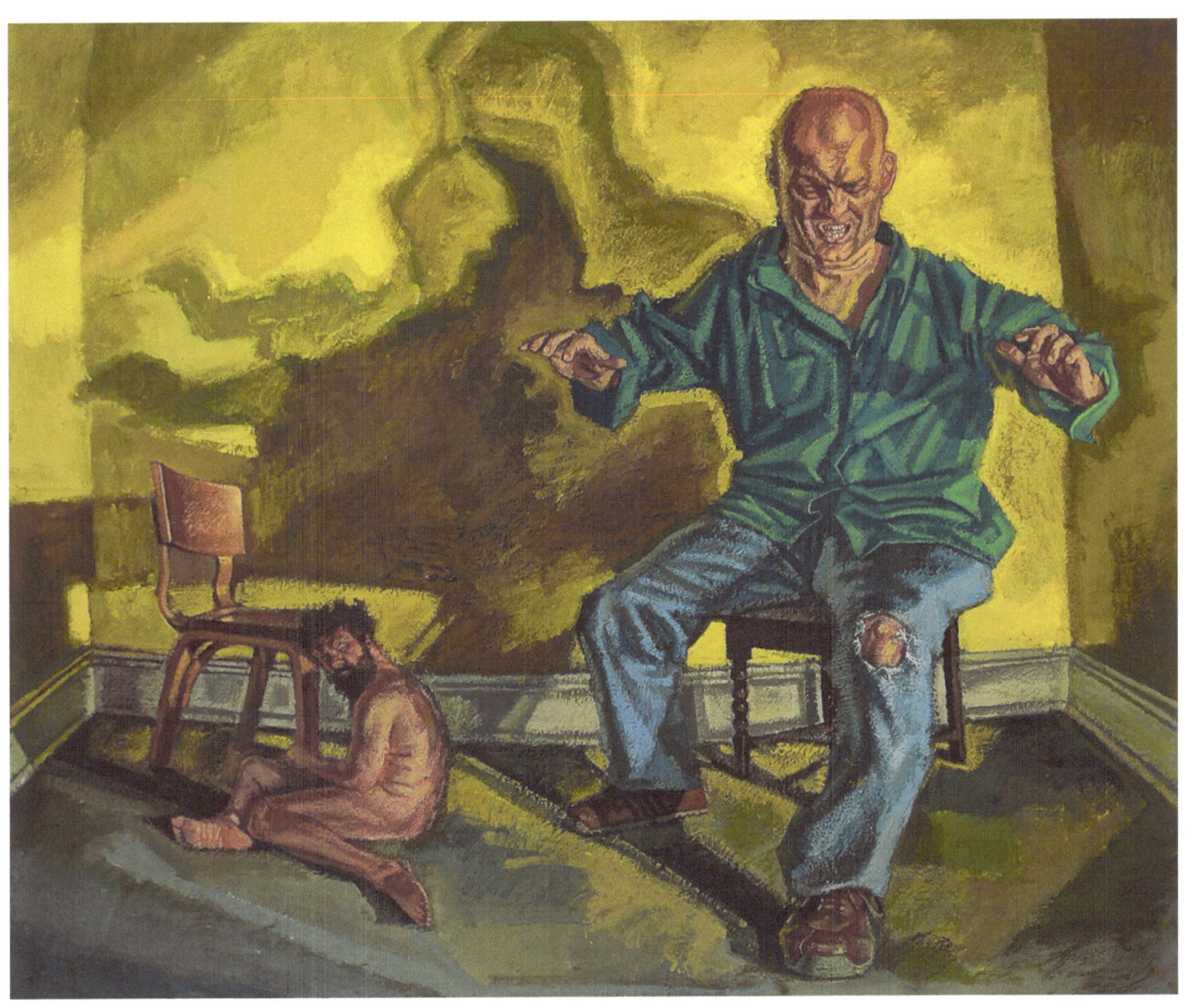

ananian, michael

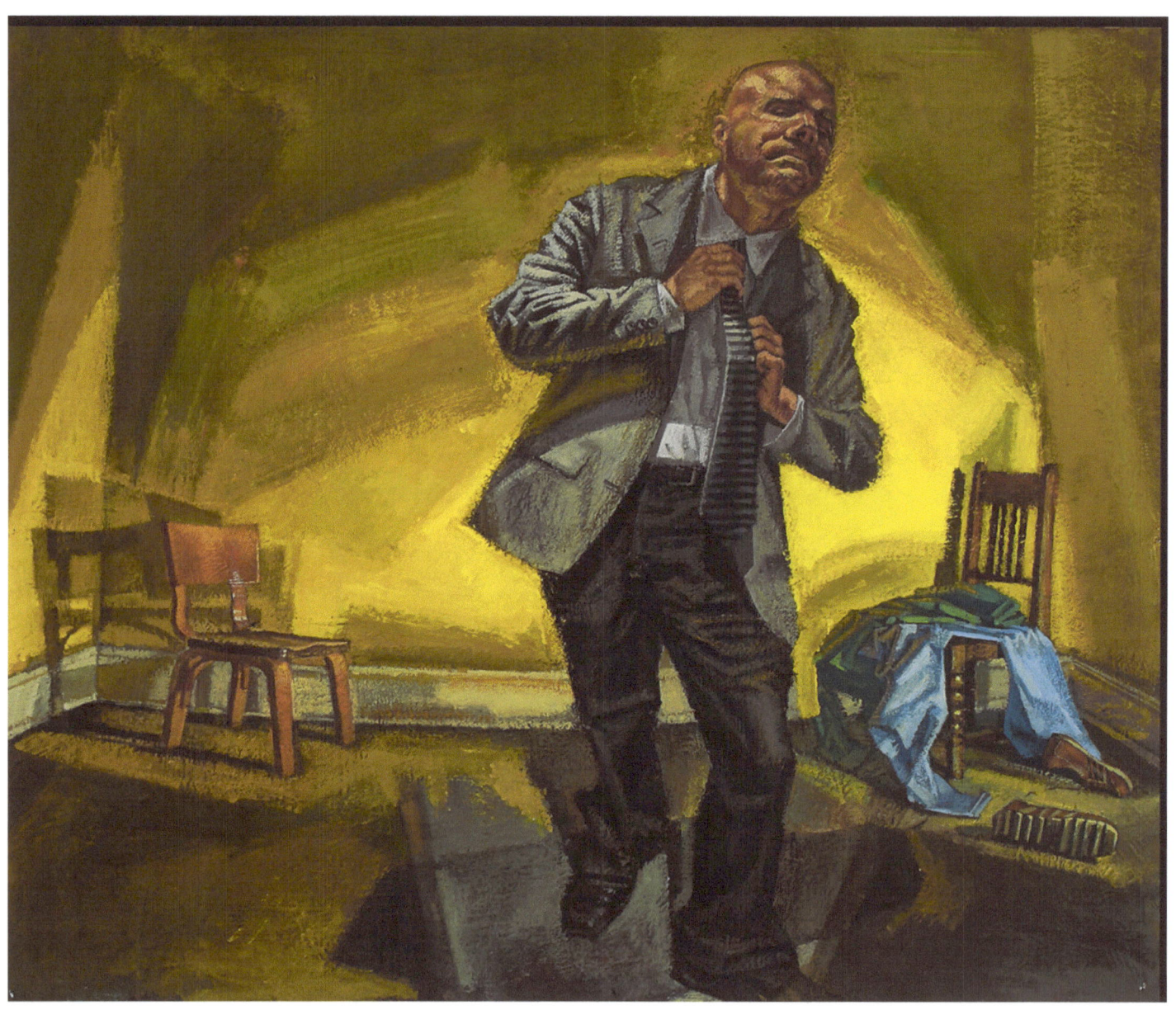

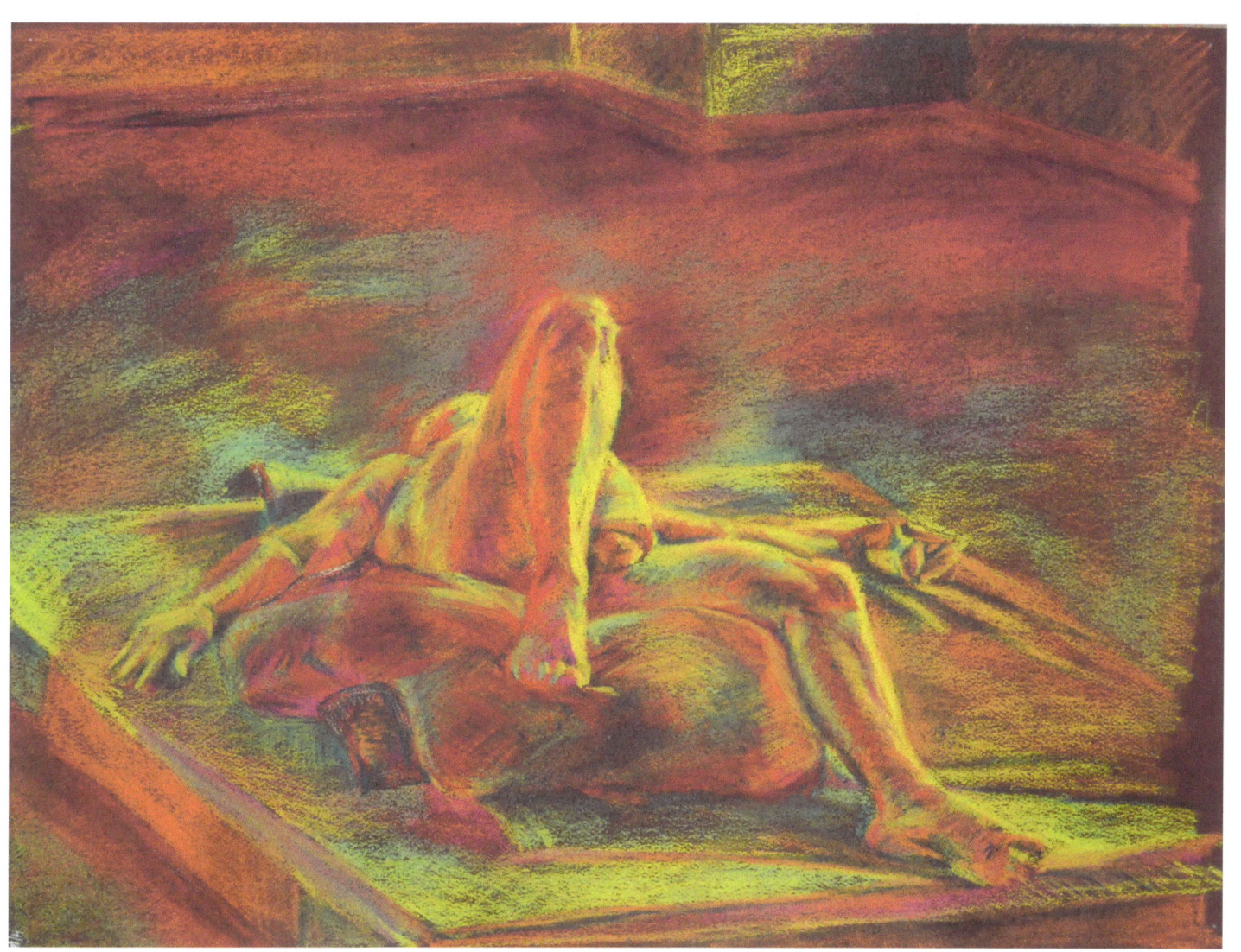

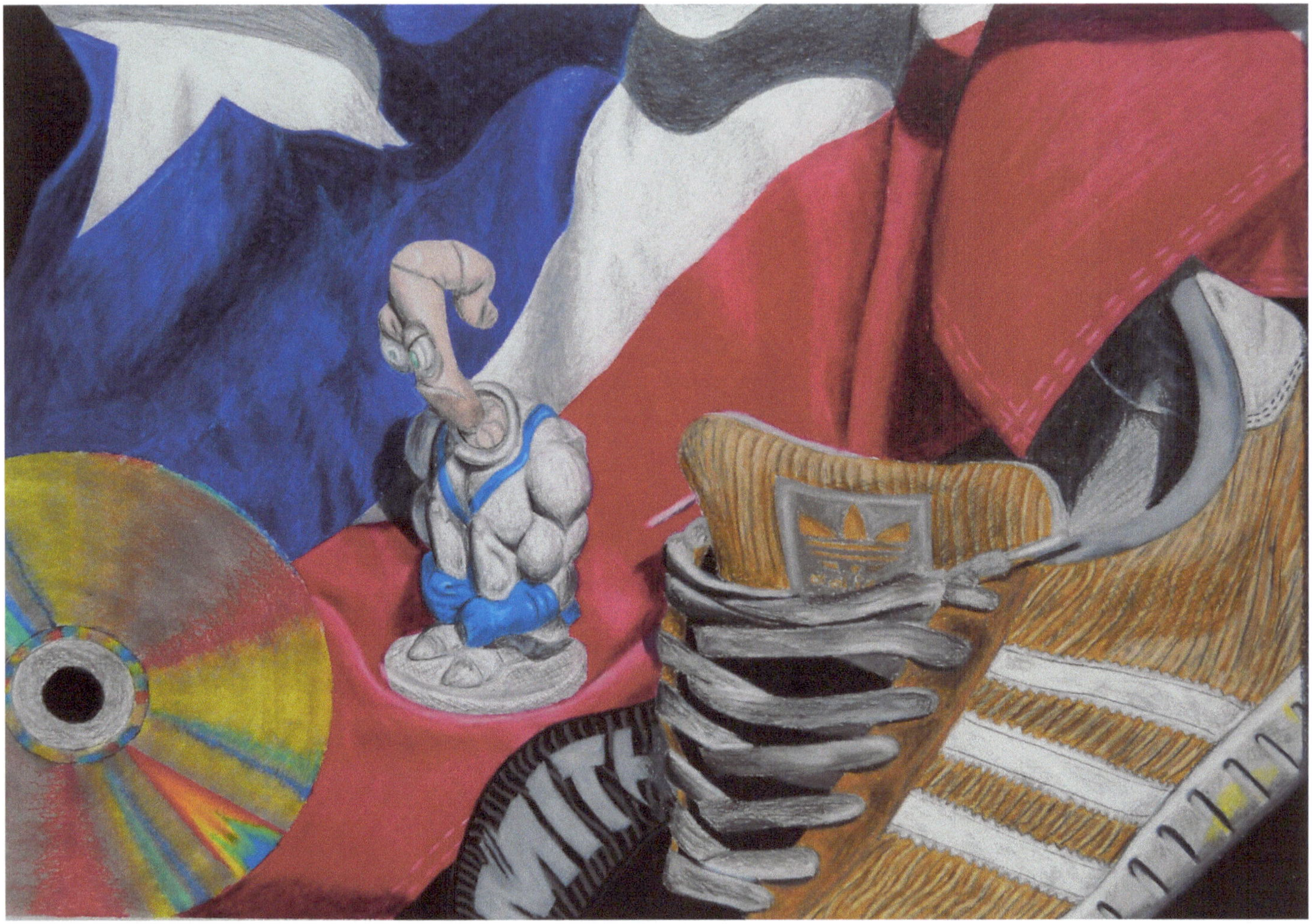

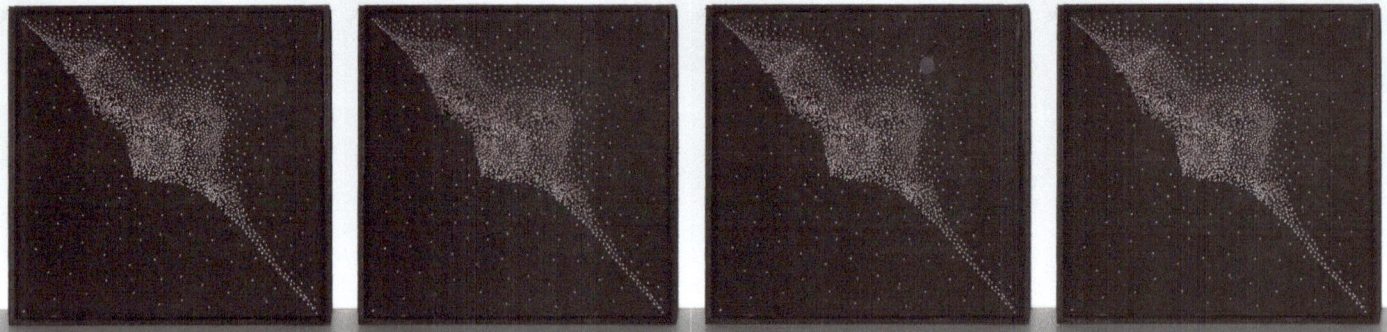

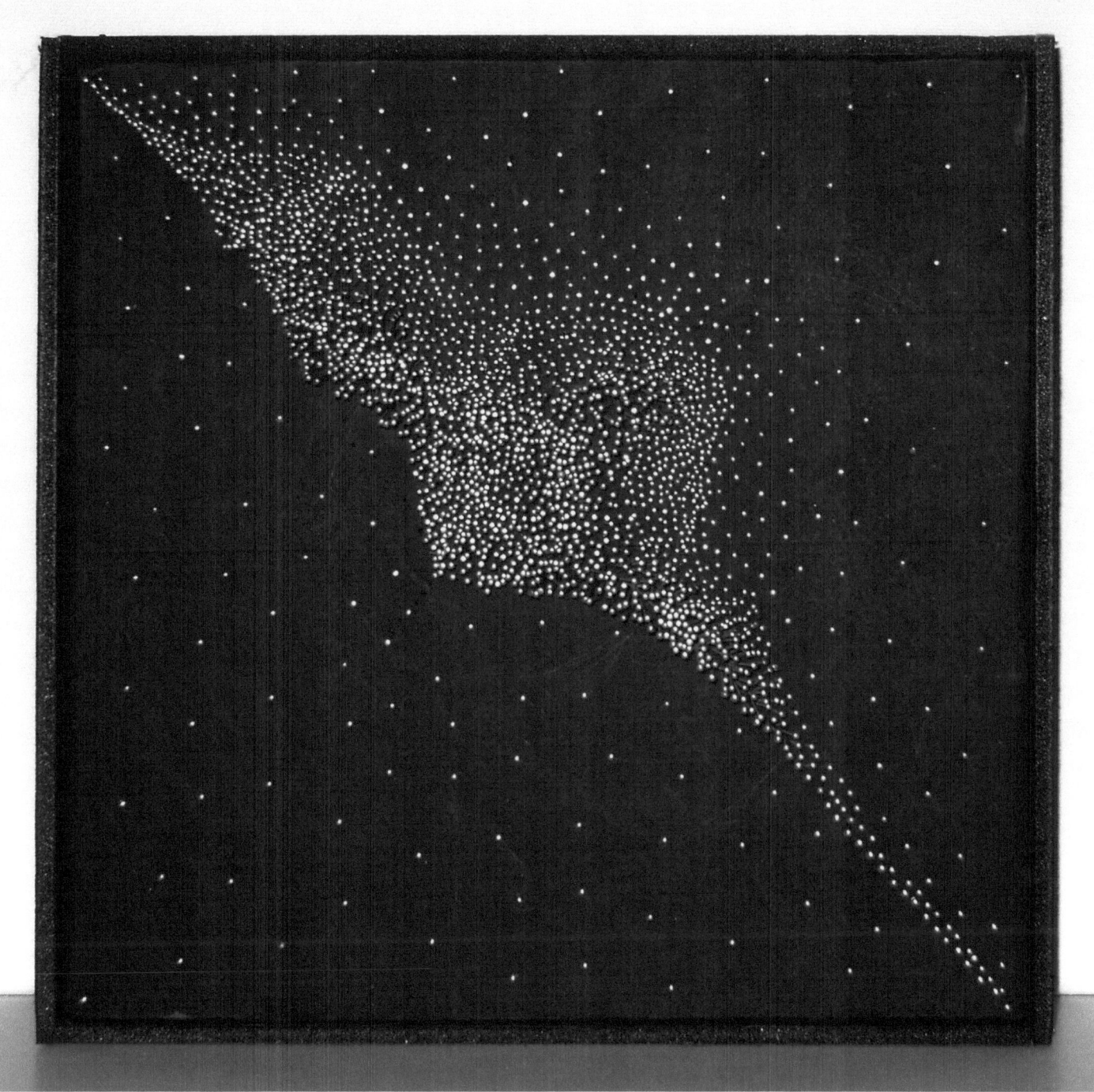

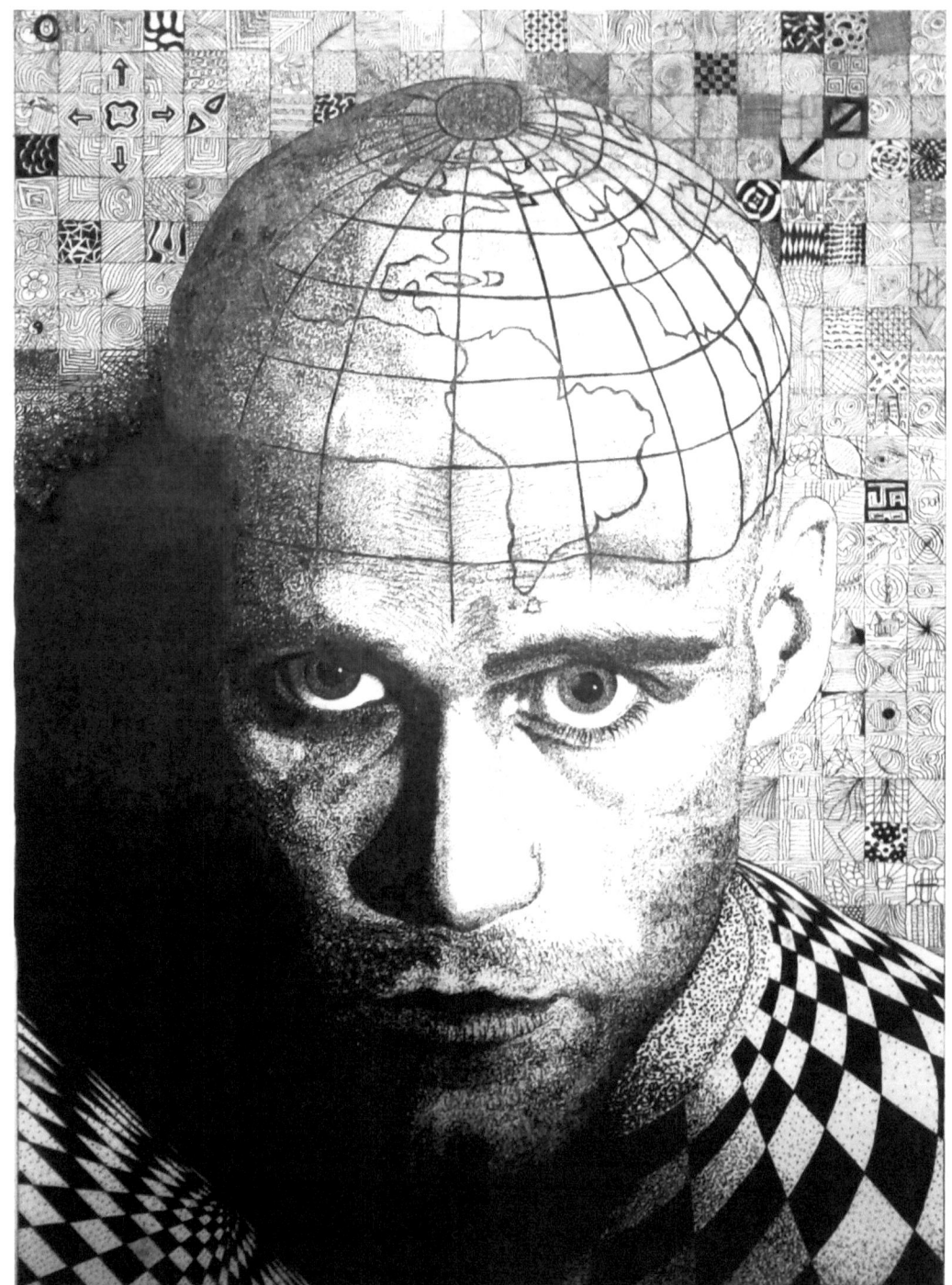

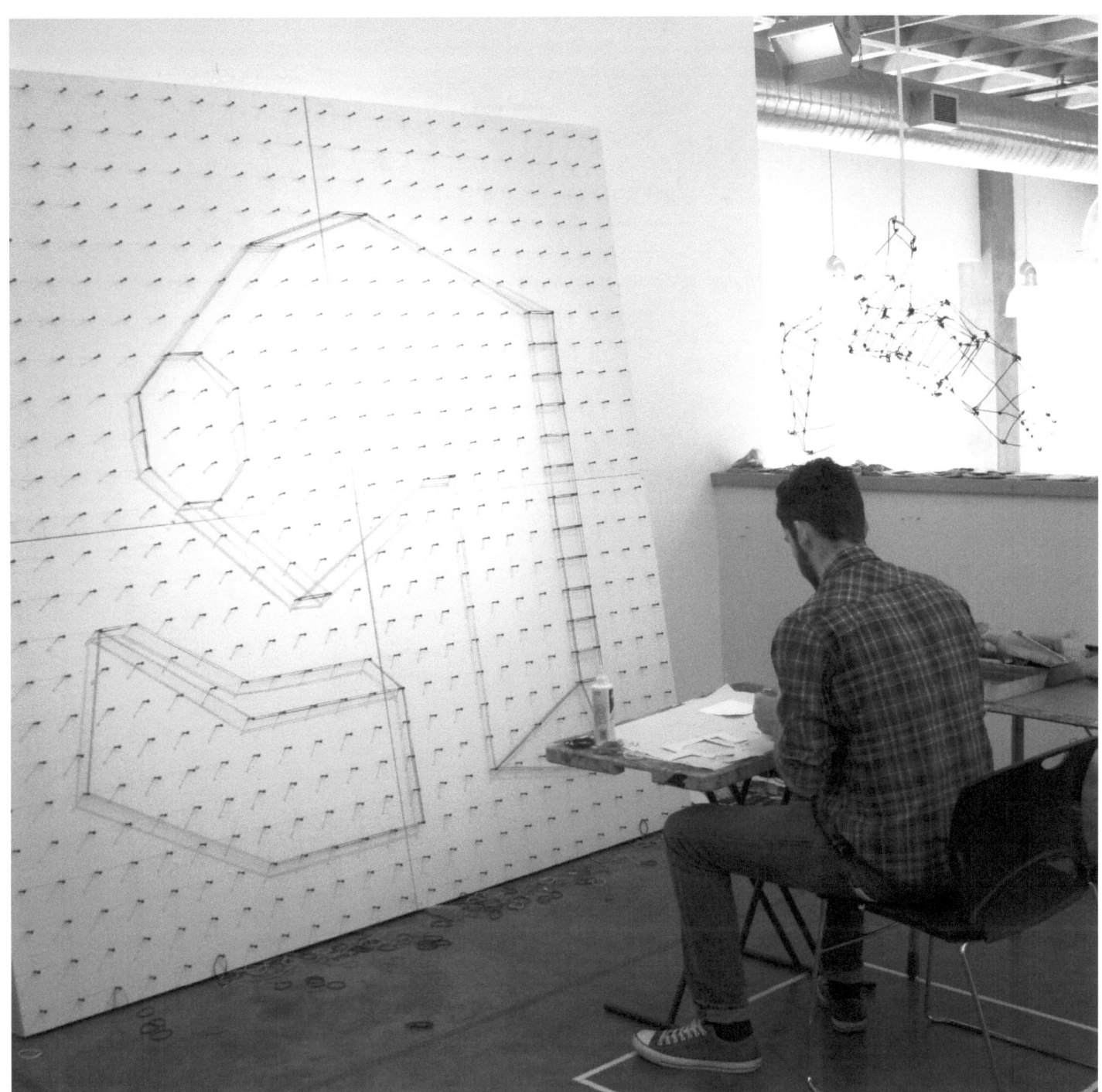

mckenzie, alex

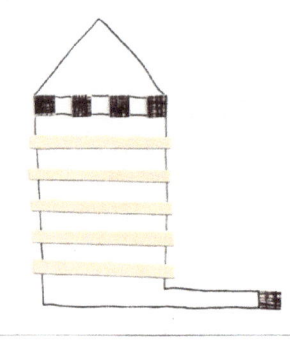 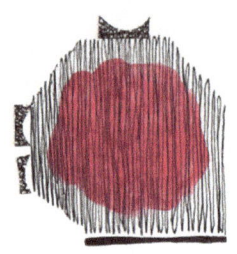 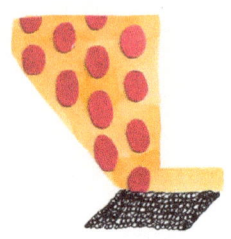
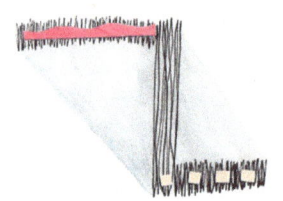 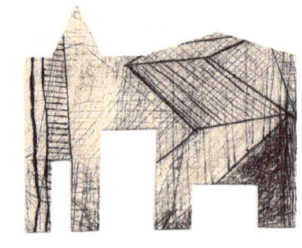 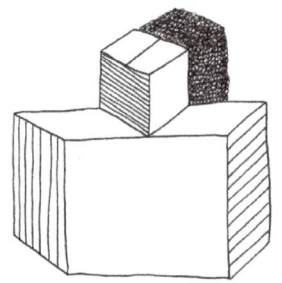
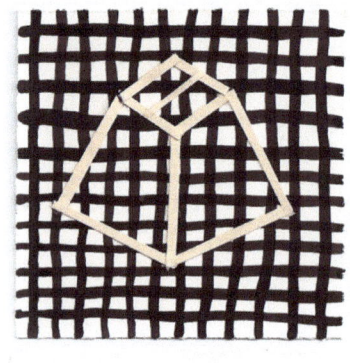 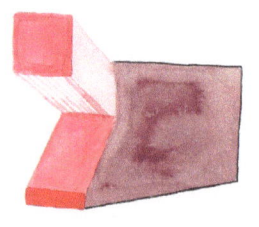 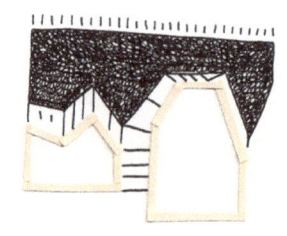
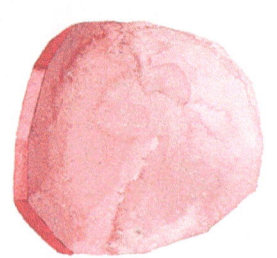 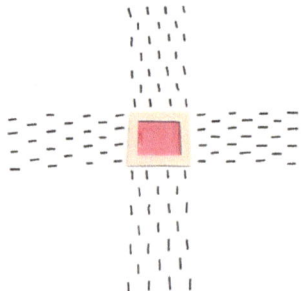

mckenzie, alex

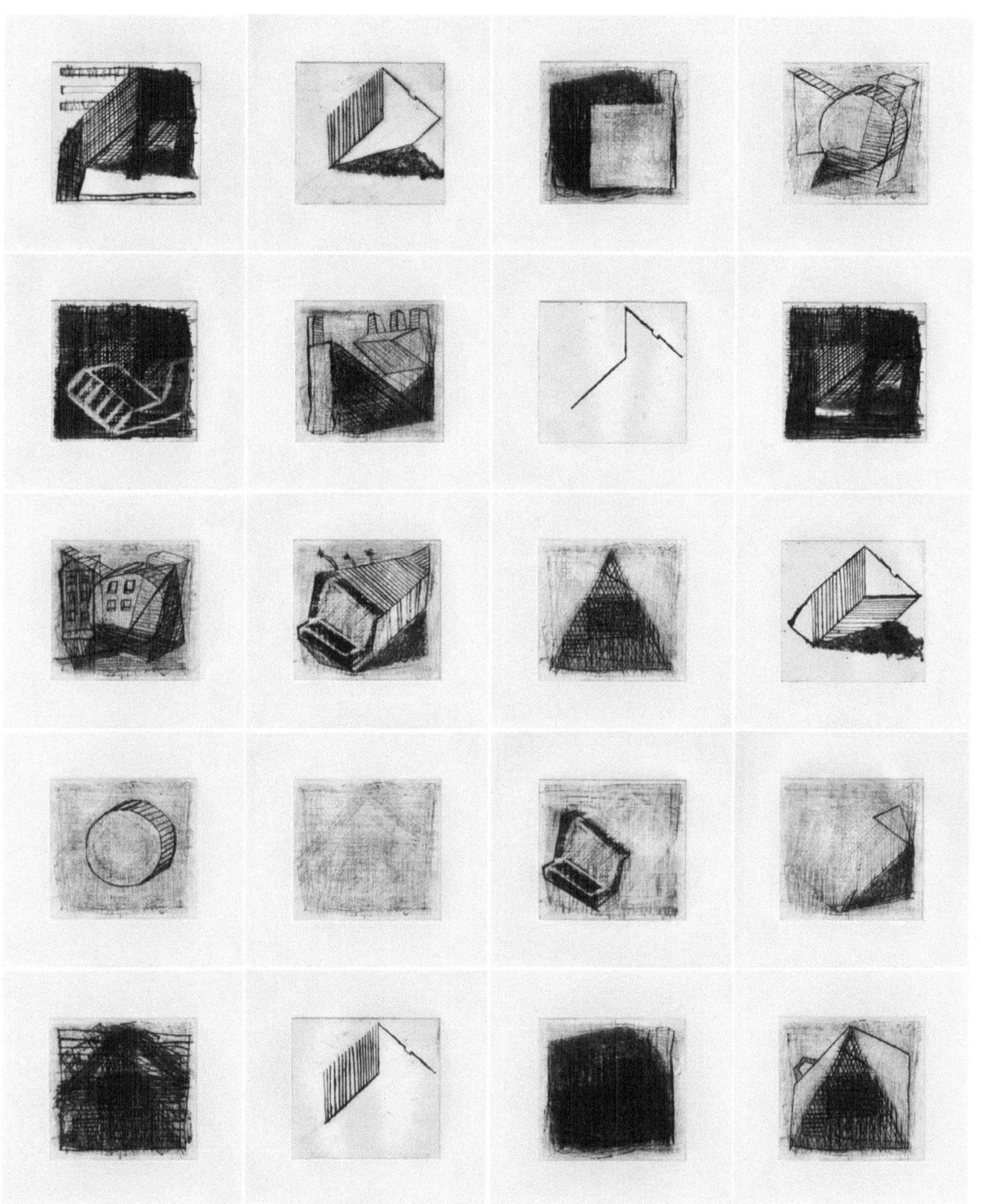

mckenzie, alex

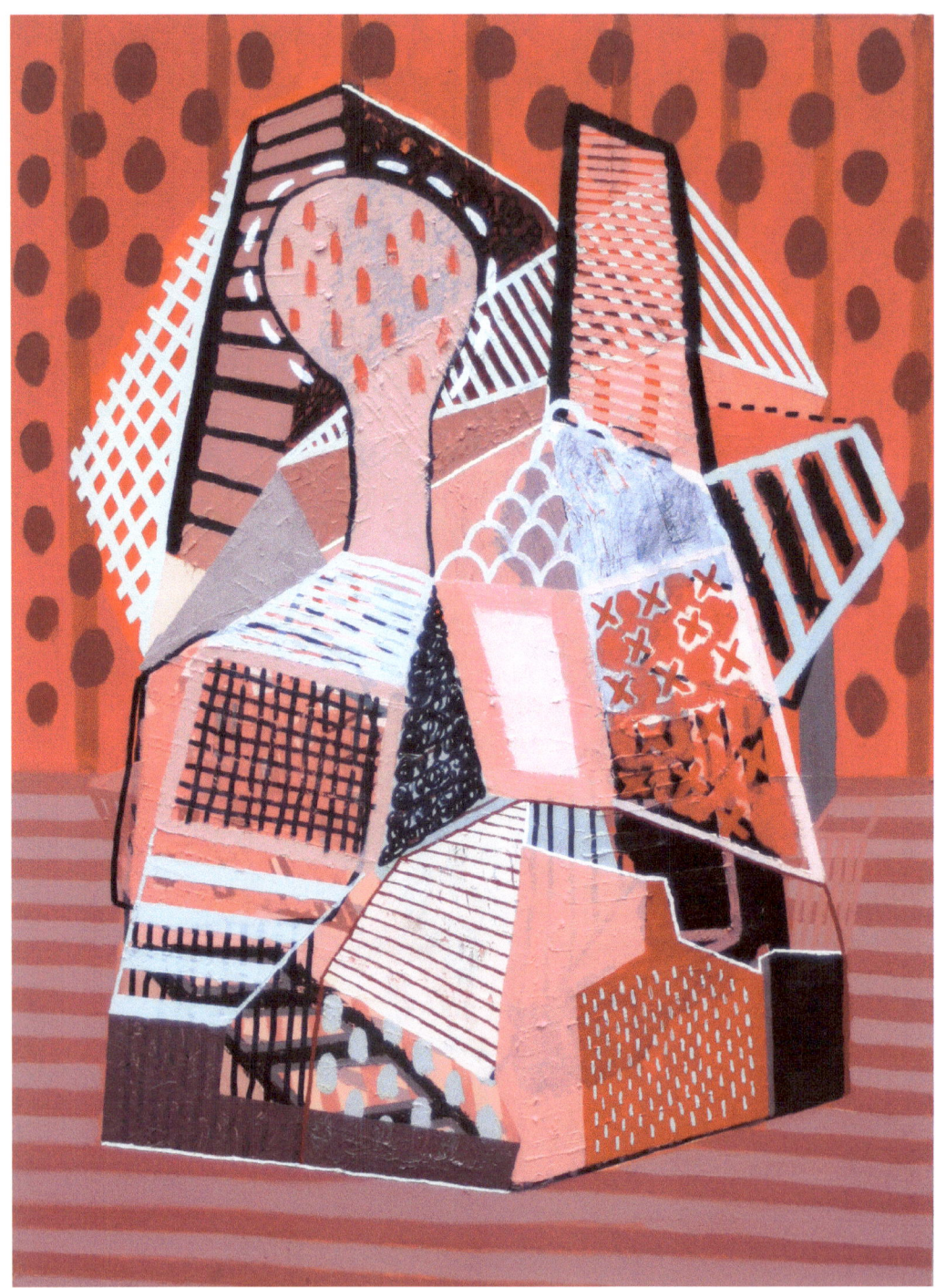

mckenzie, alex

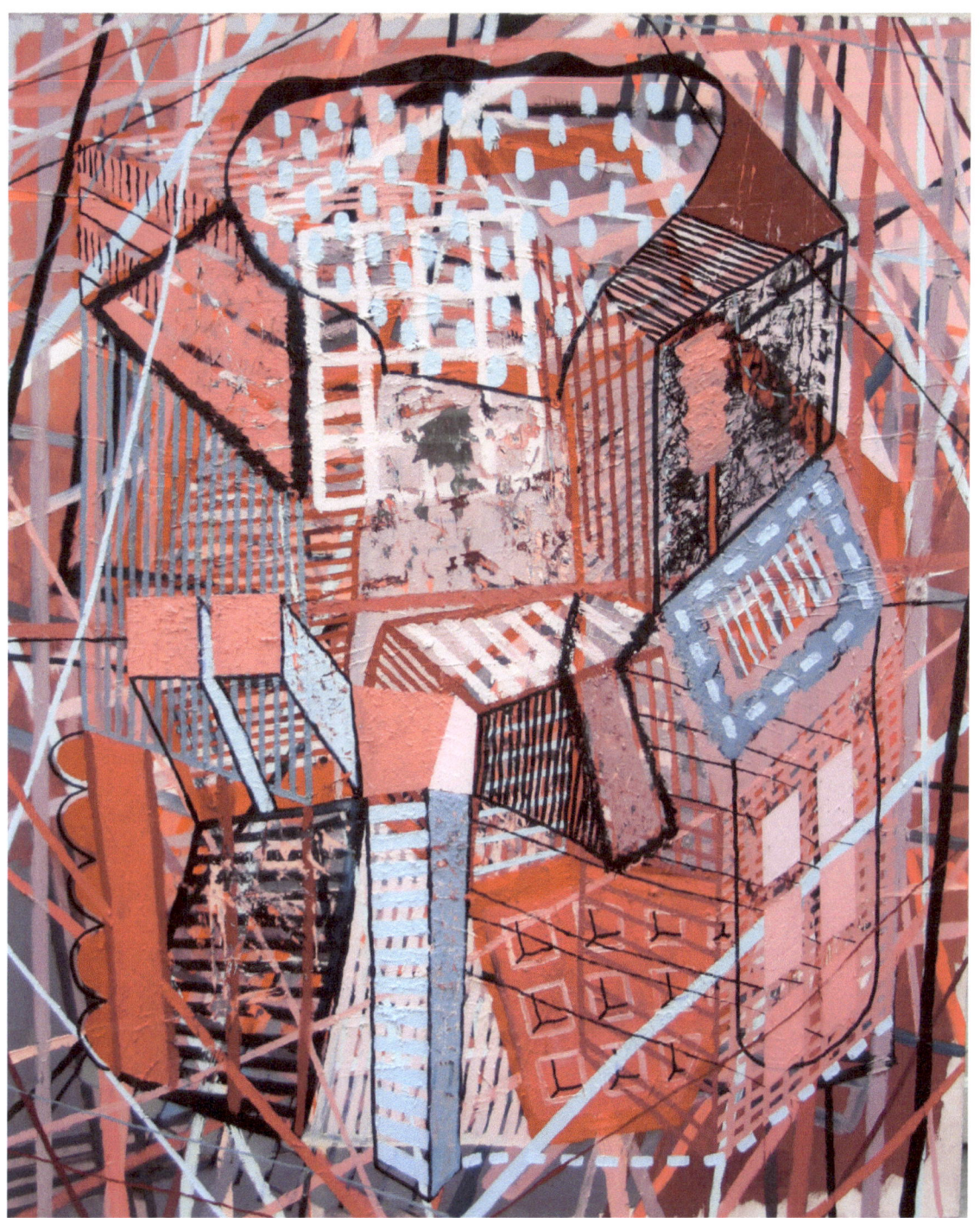

mckenzie, alex

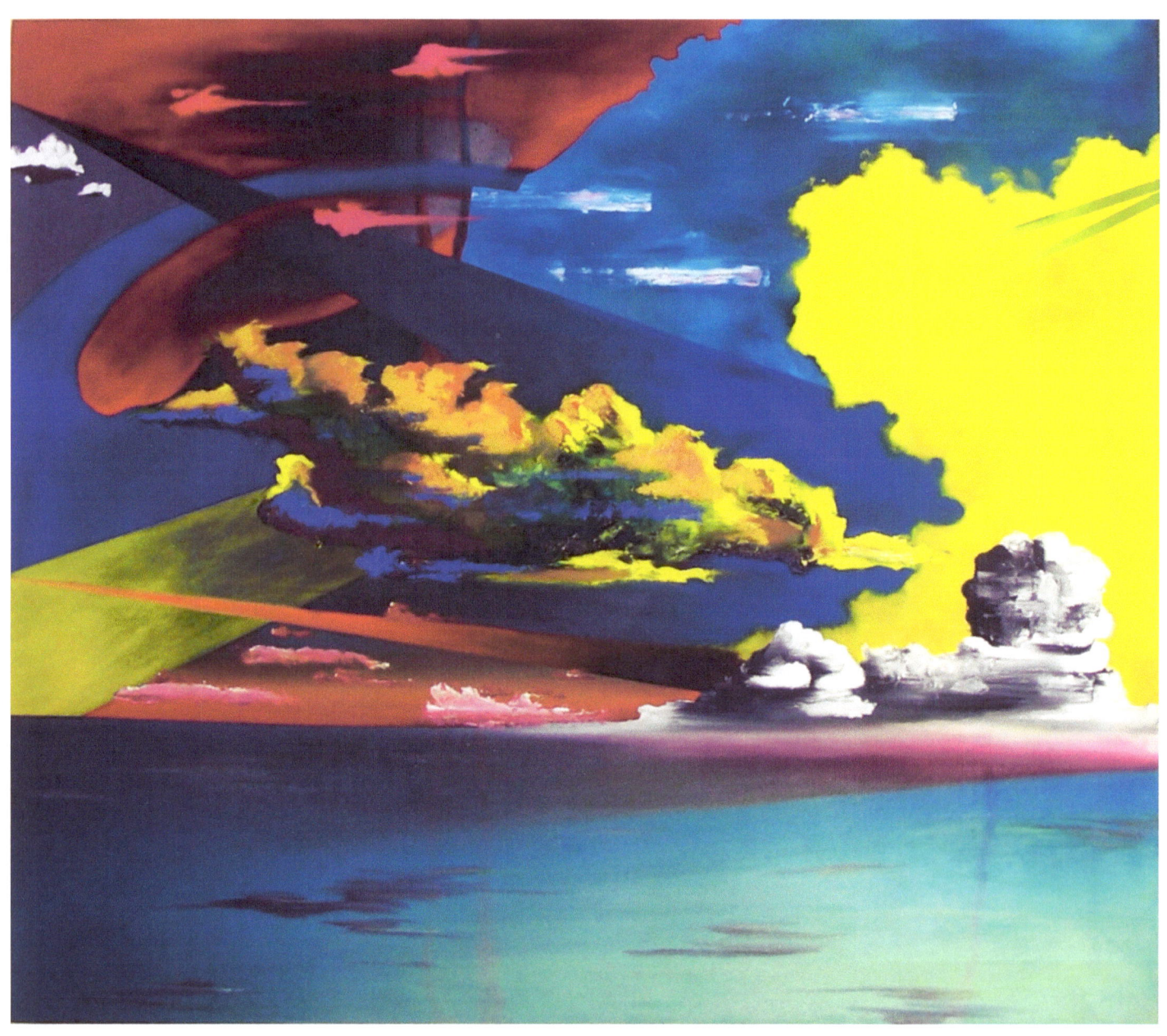

morris, christopher h

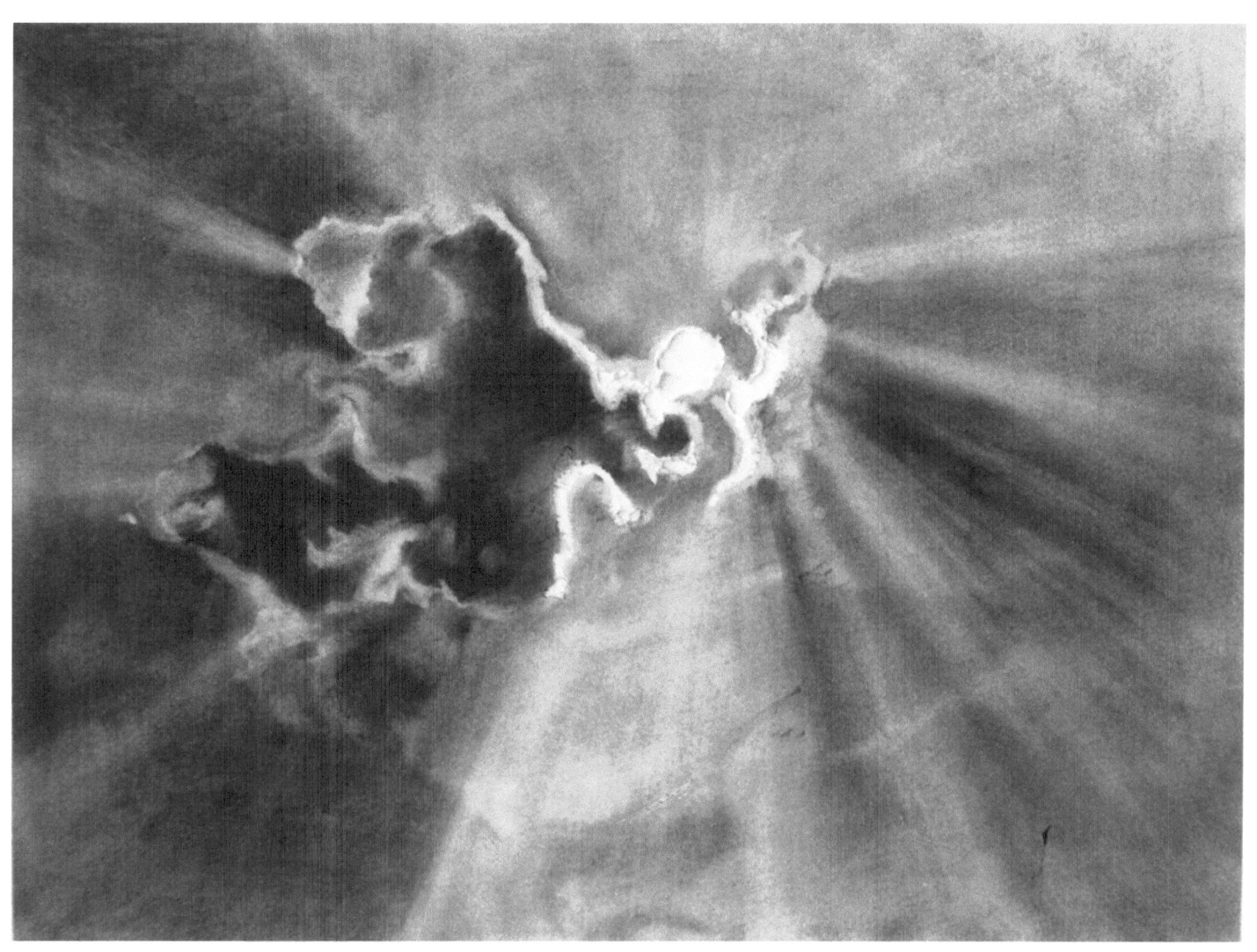

morris, christopher h

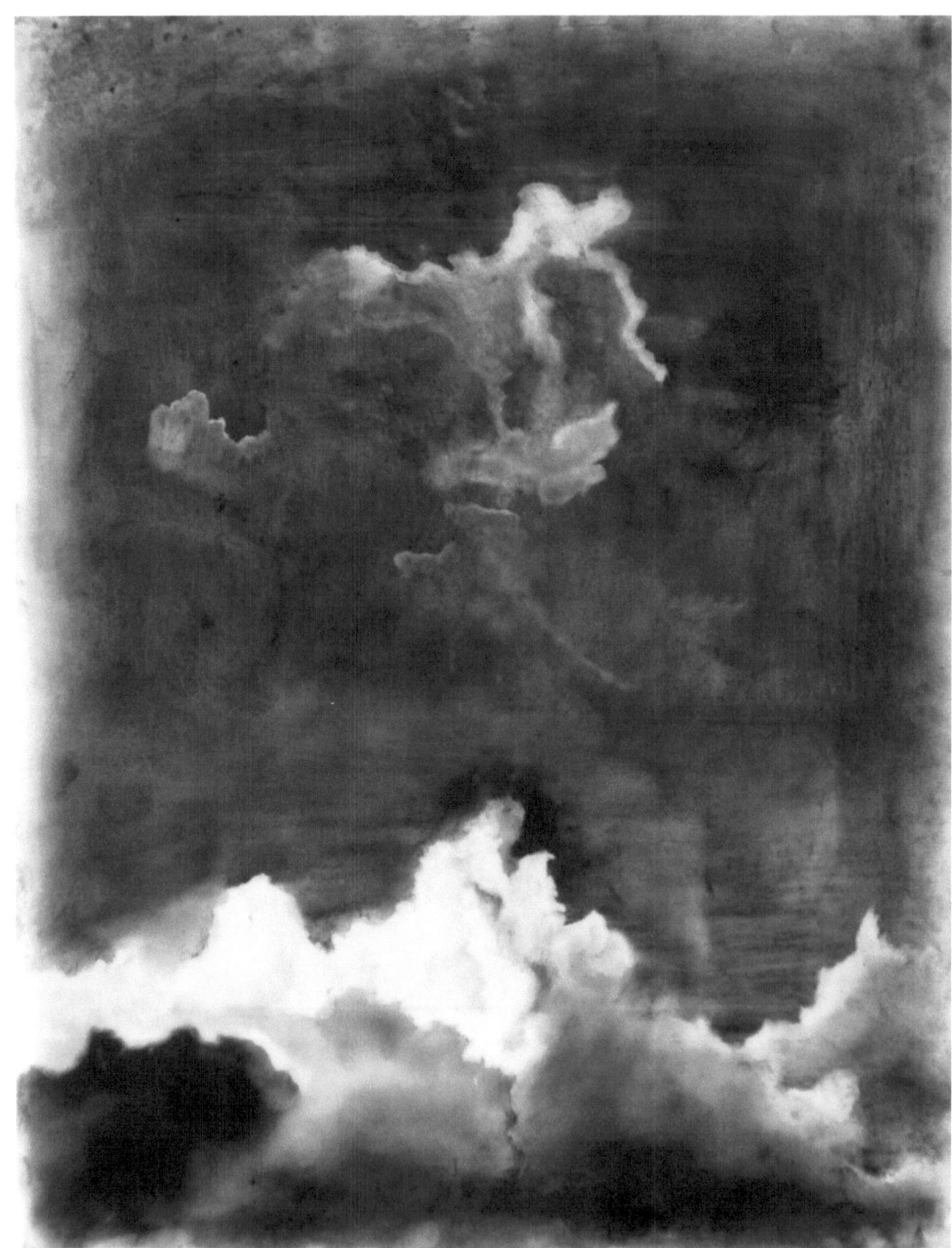

morris, christopher h

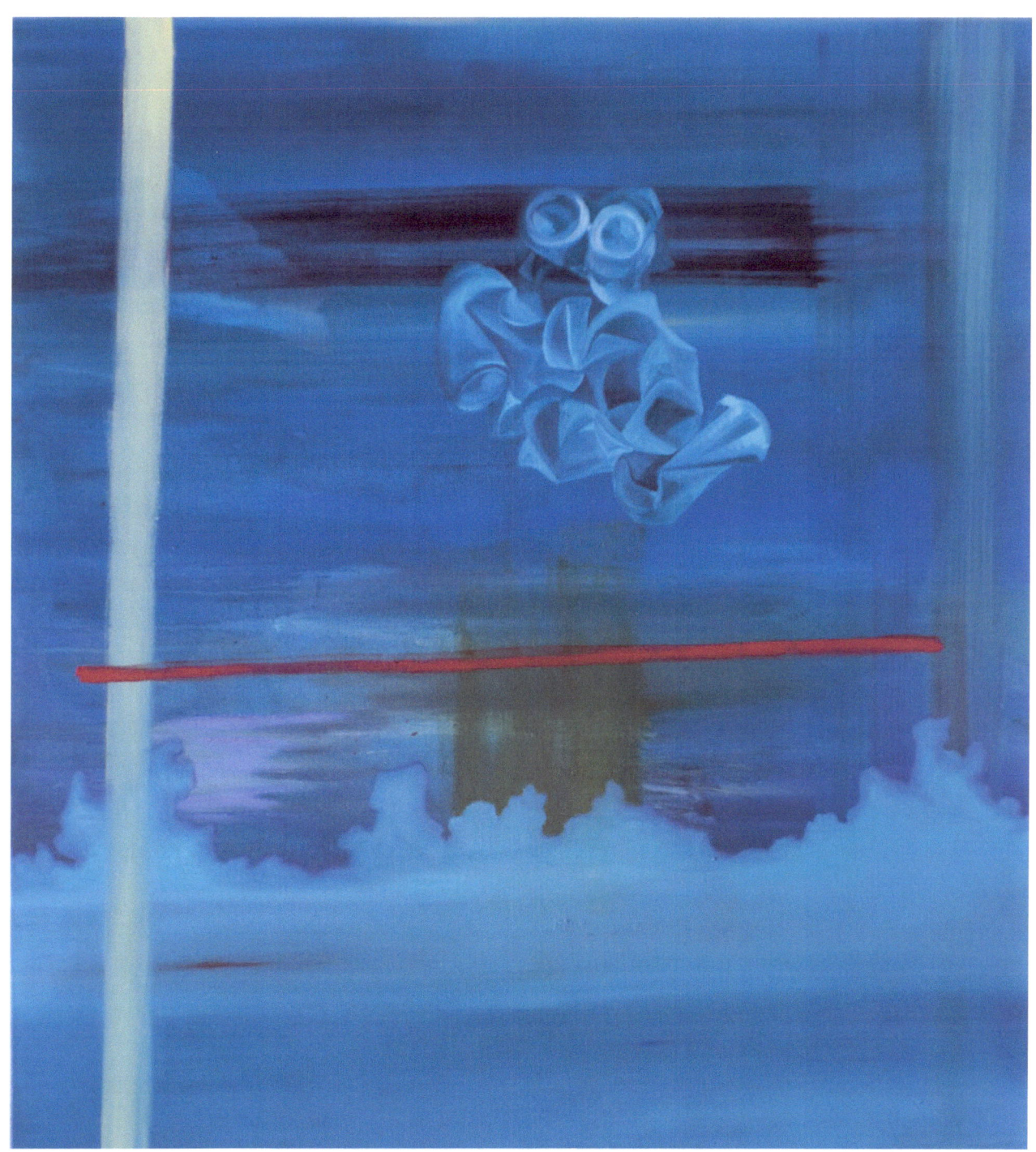

morris, christopher h

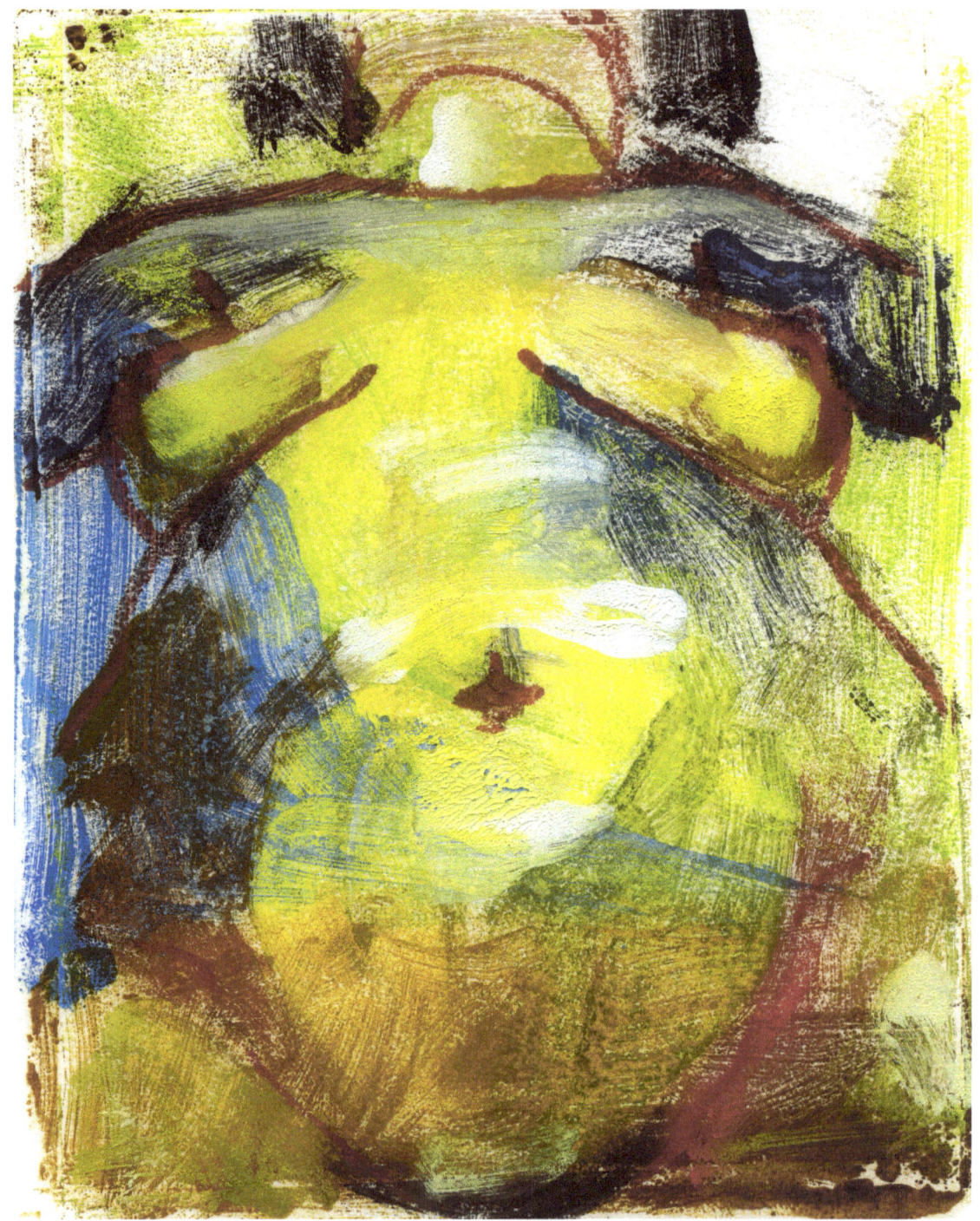

pintado, steisha

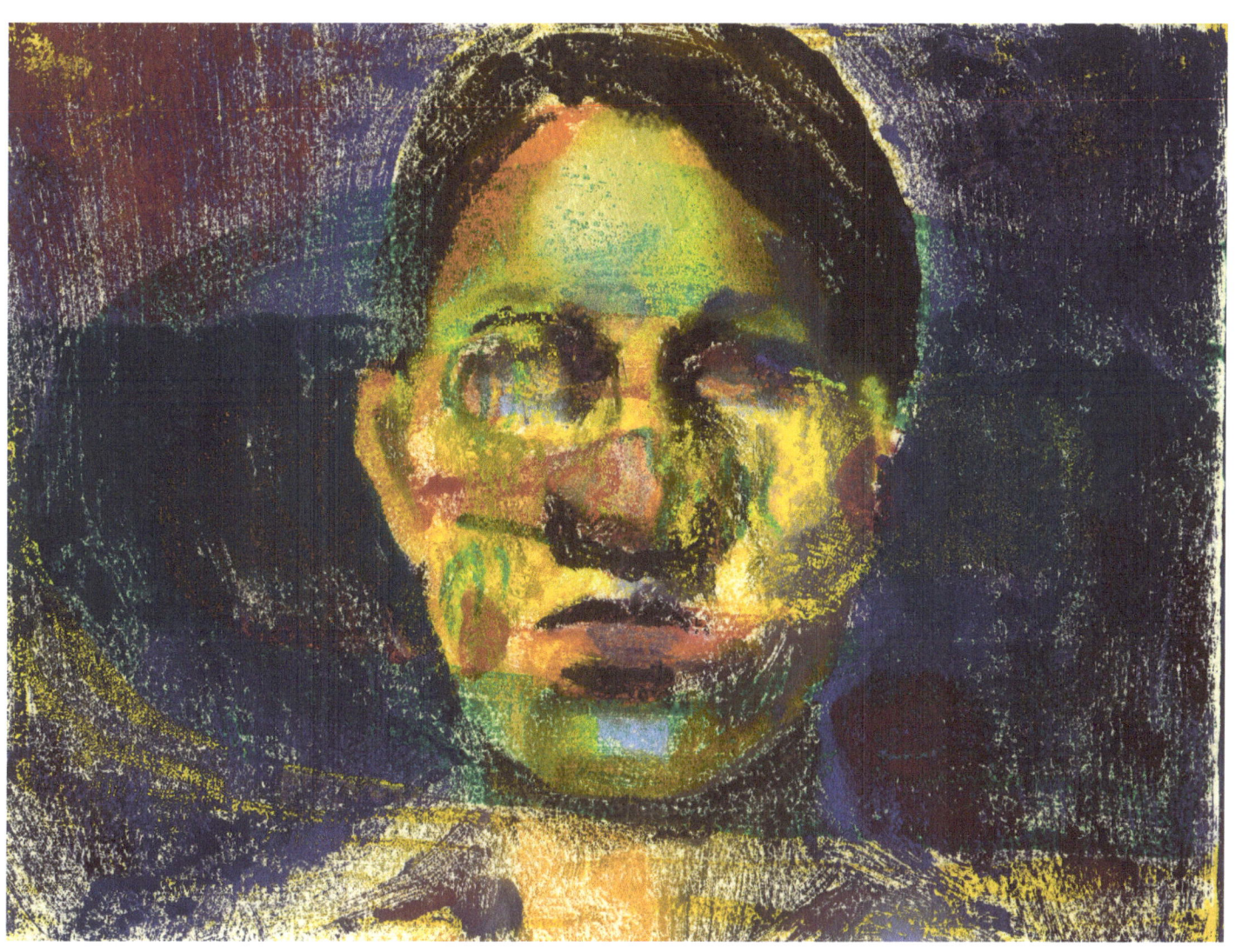

pintado, steisha

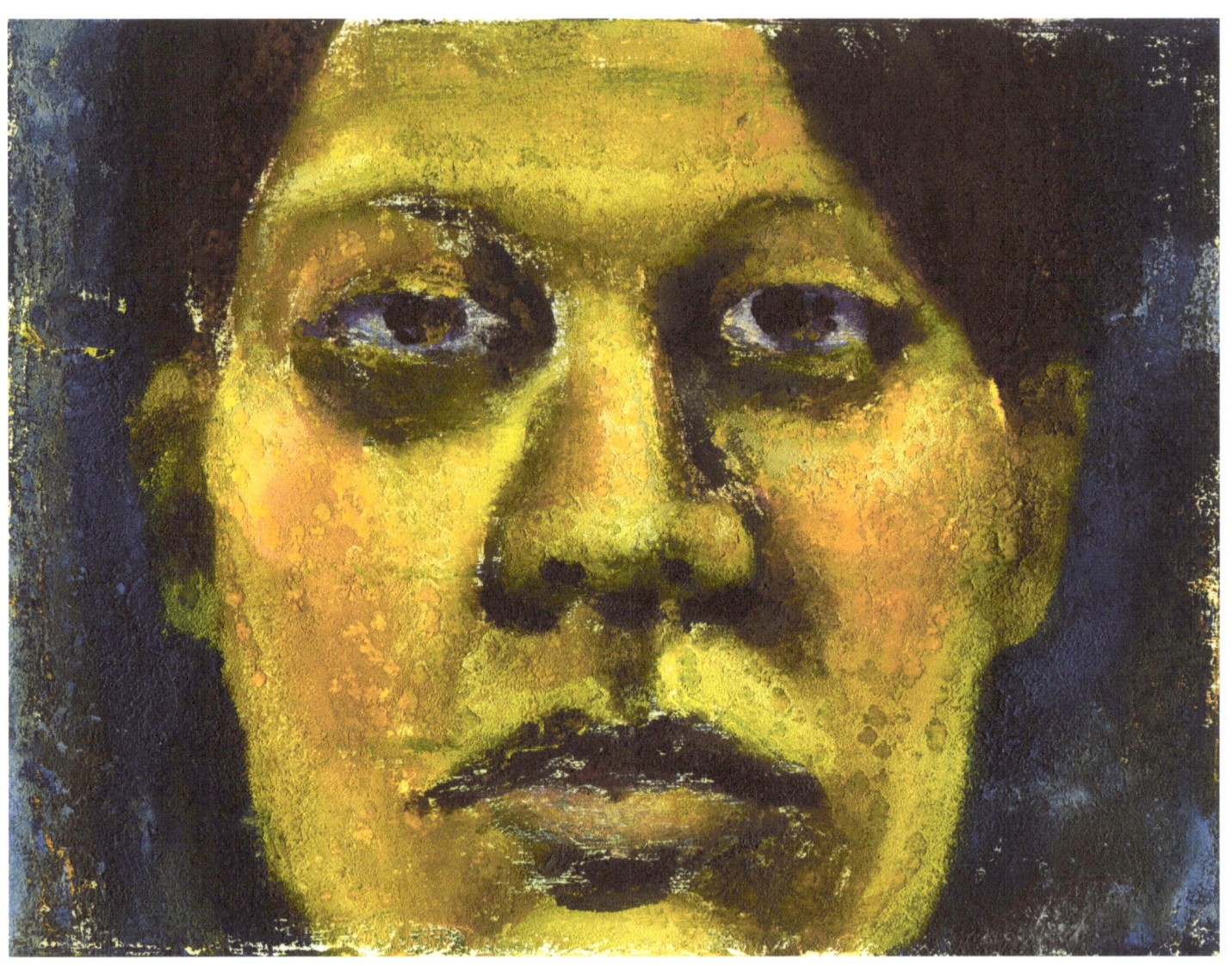

pintado, steisha

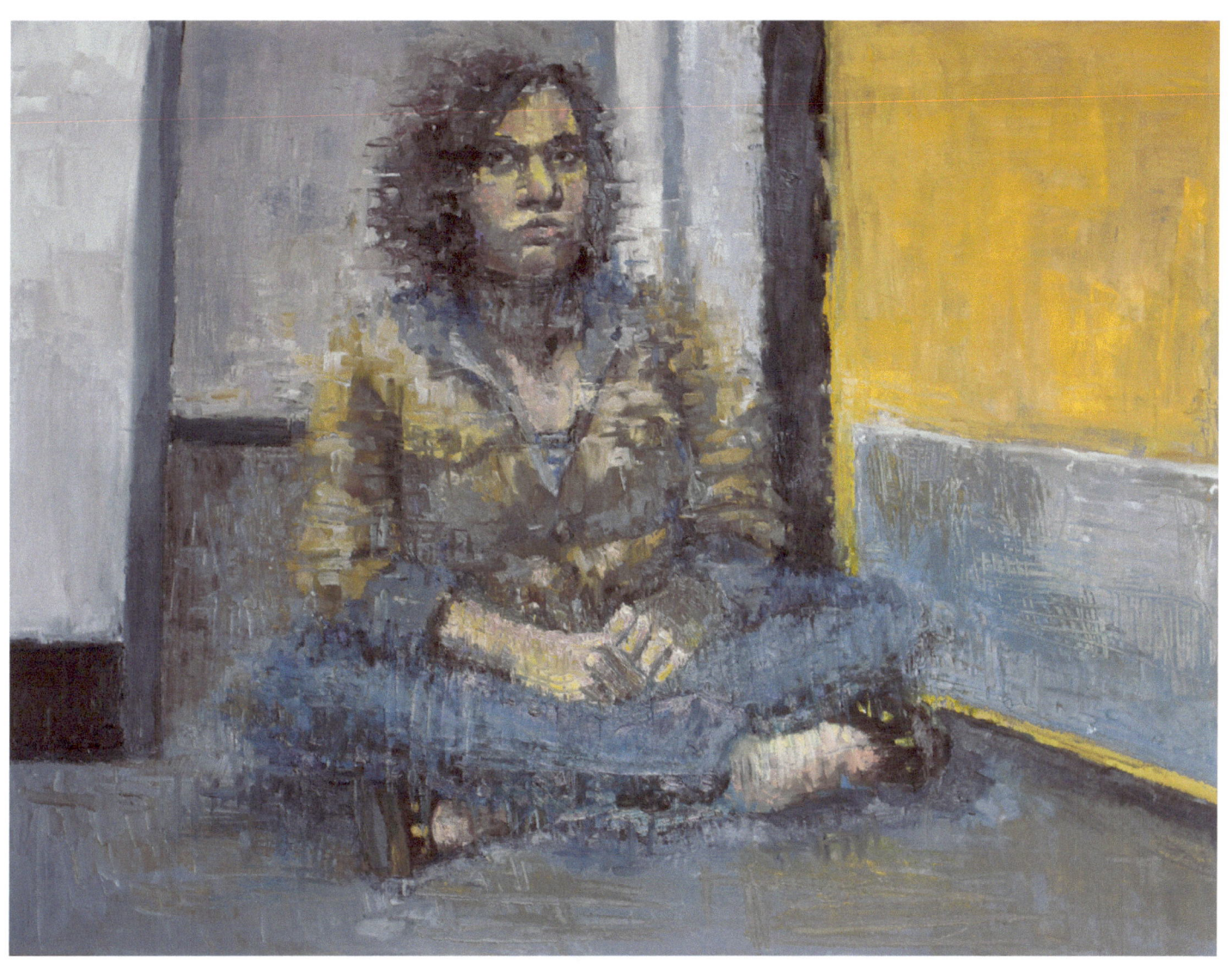

pintado, steisha

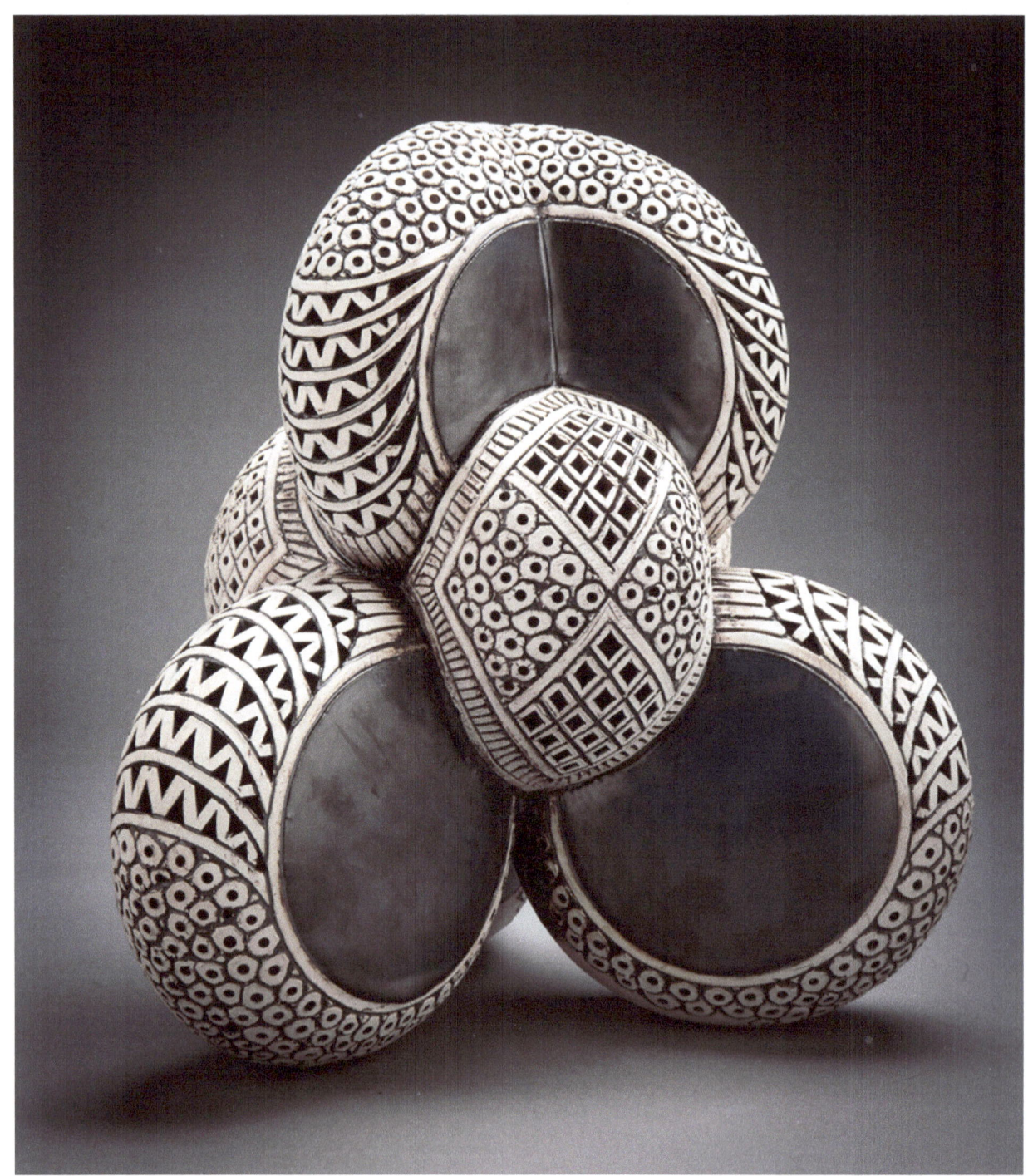

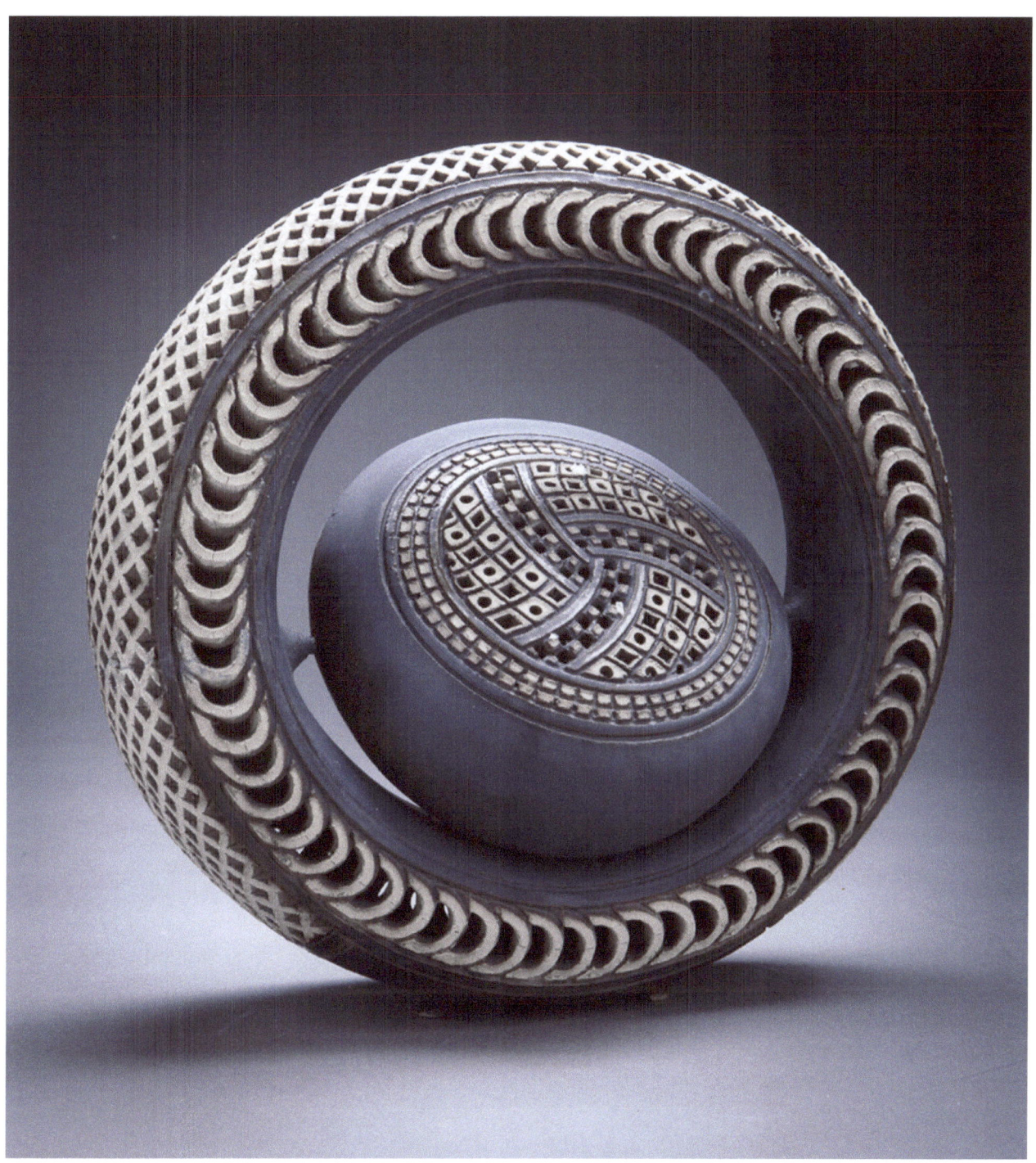

said, ibrahim

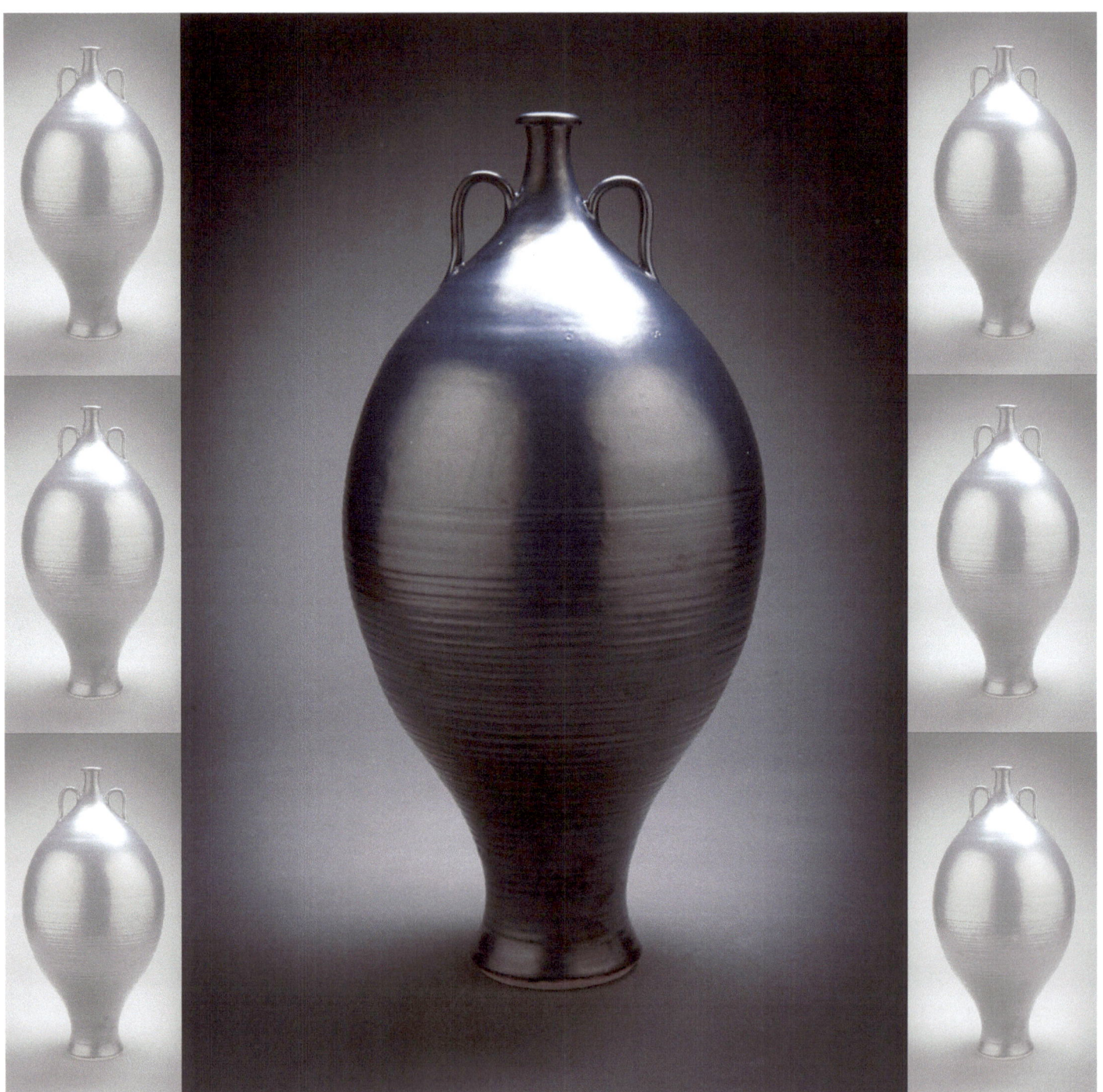

said, ibrahim

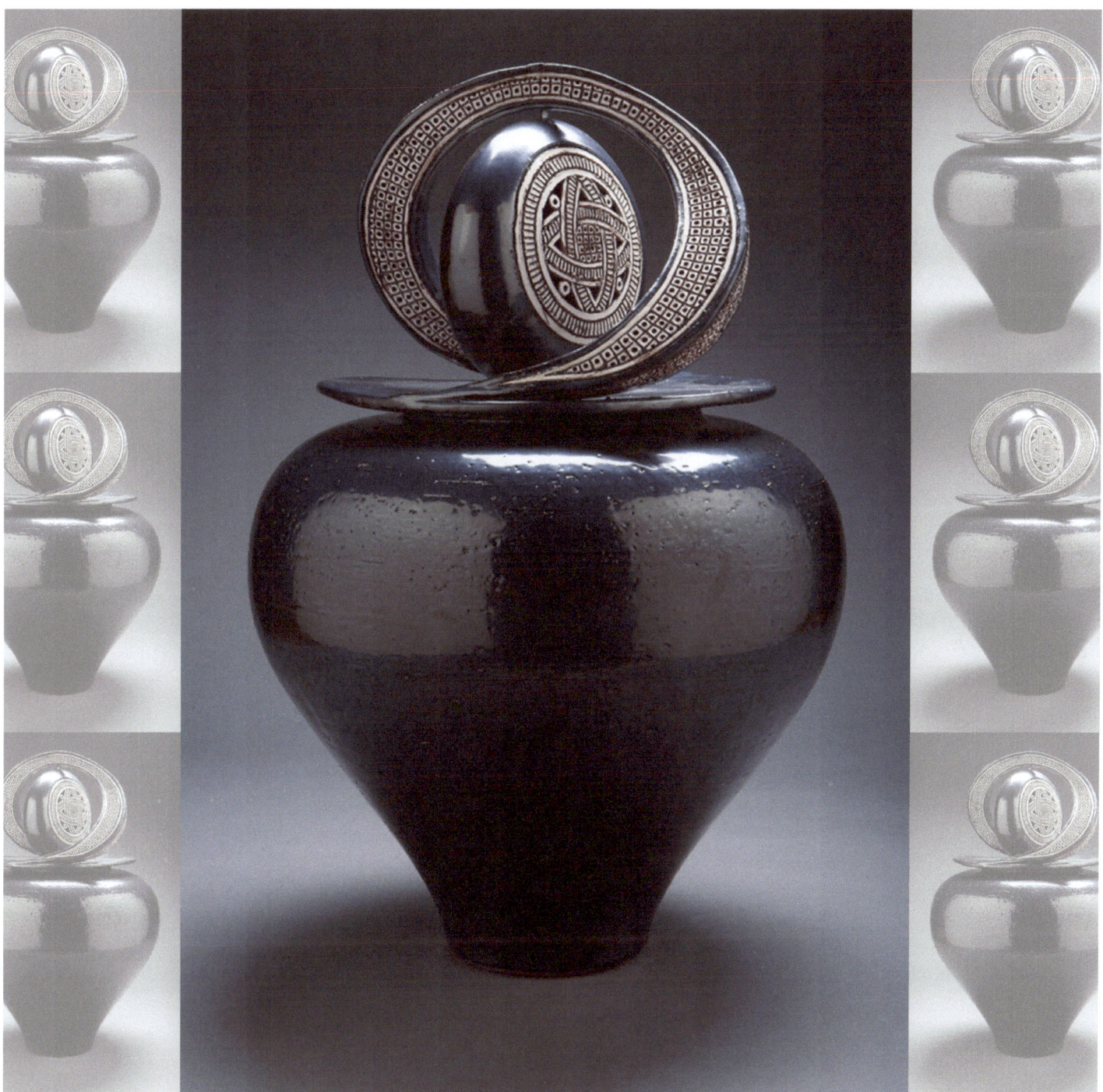

said, ibrahim

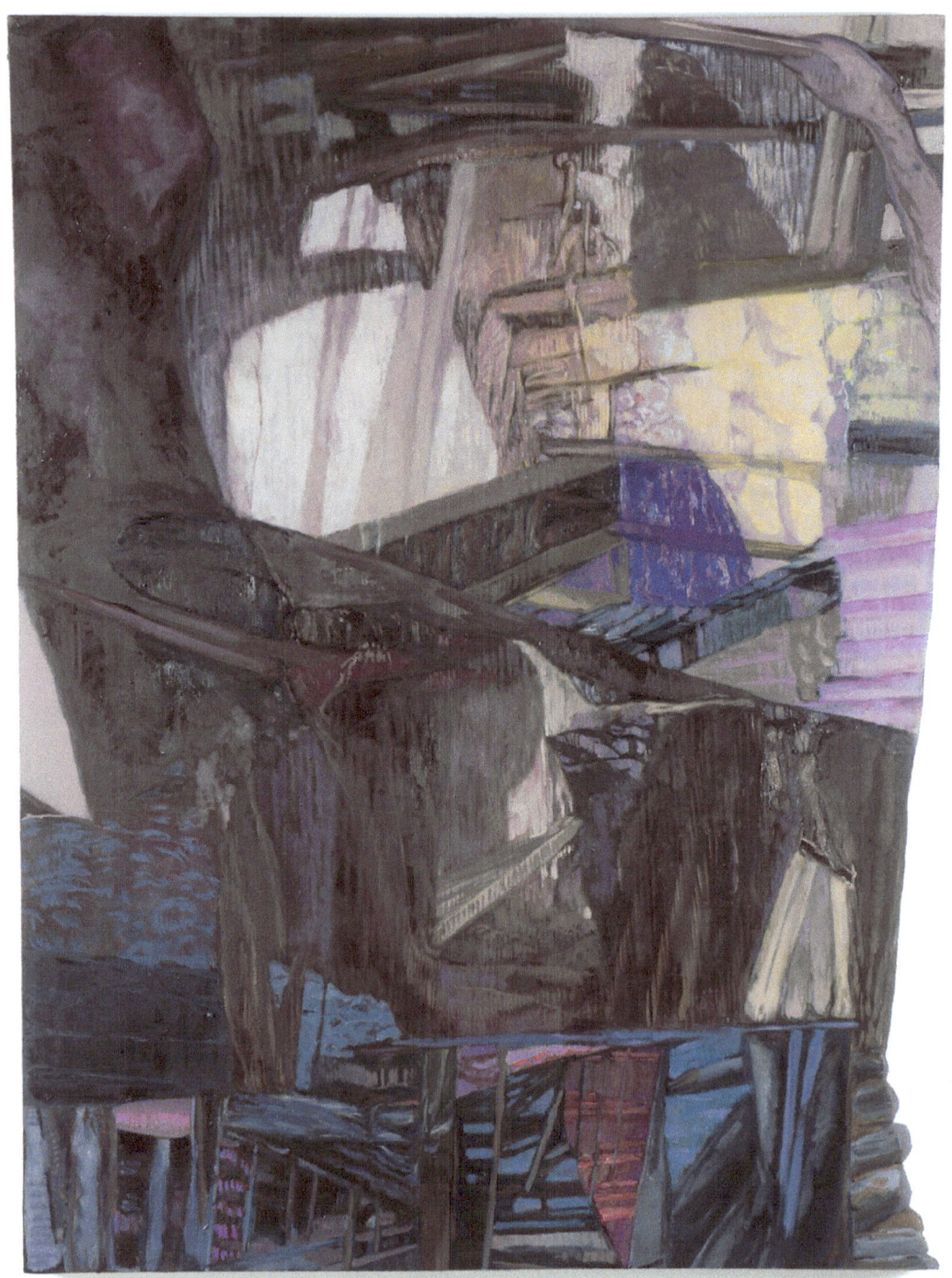

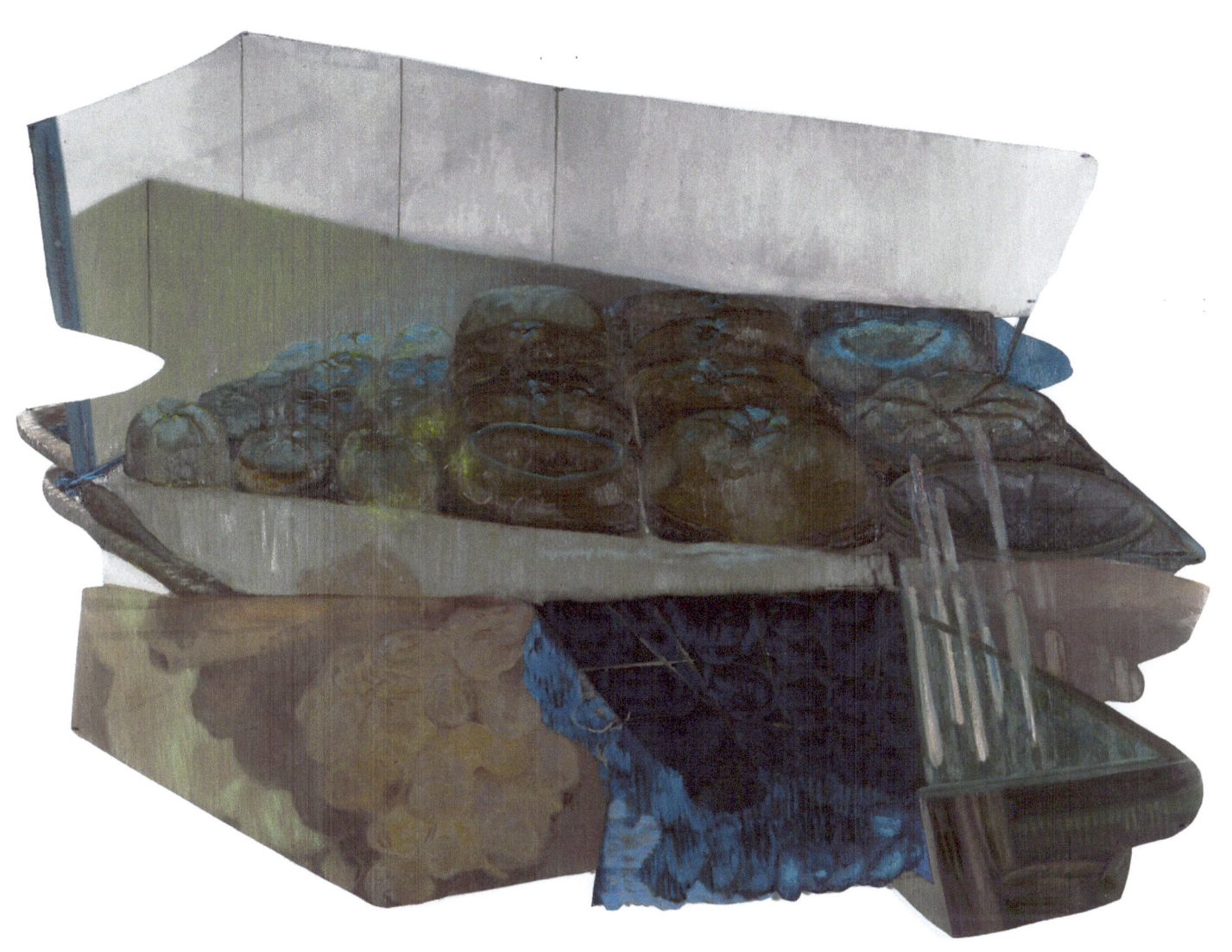

stephan, mariam

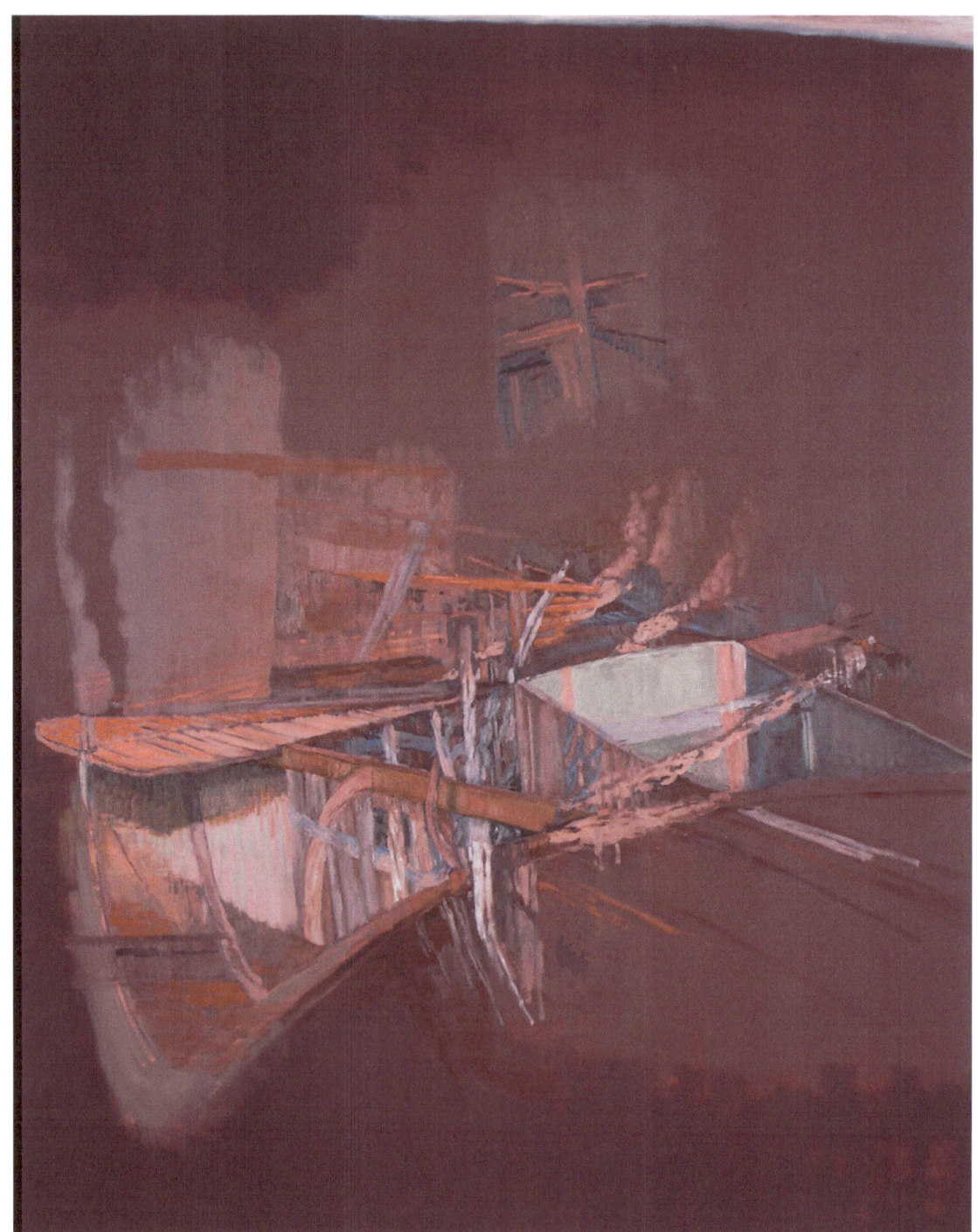

stephan, mariam

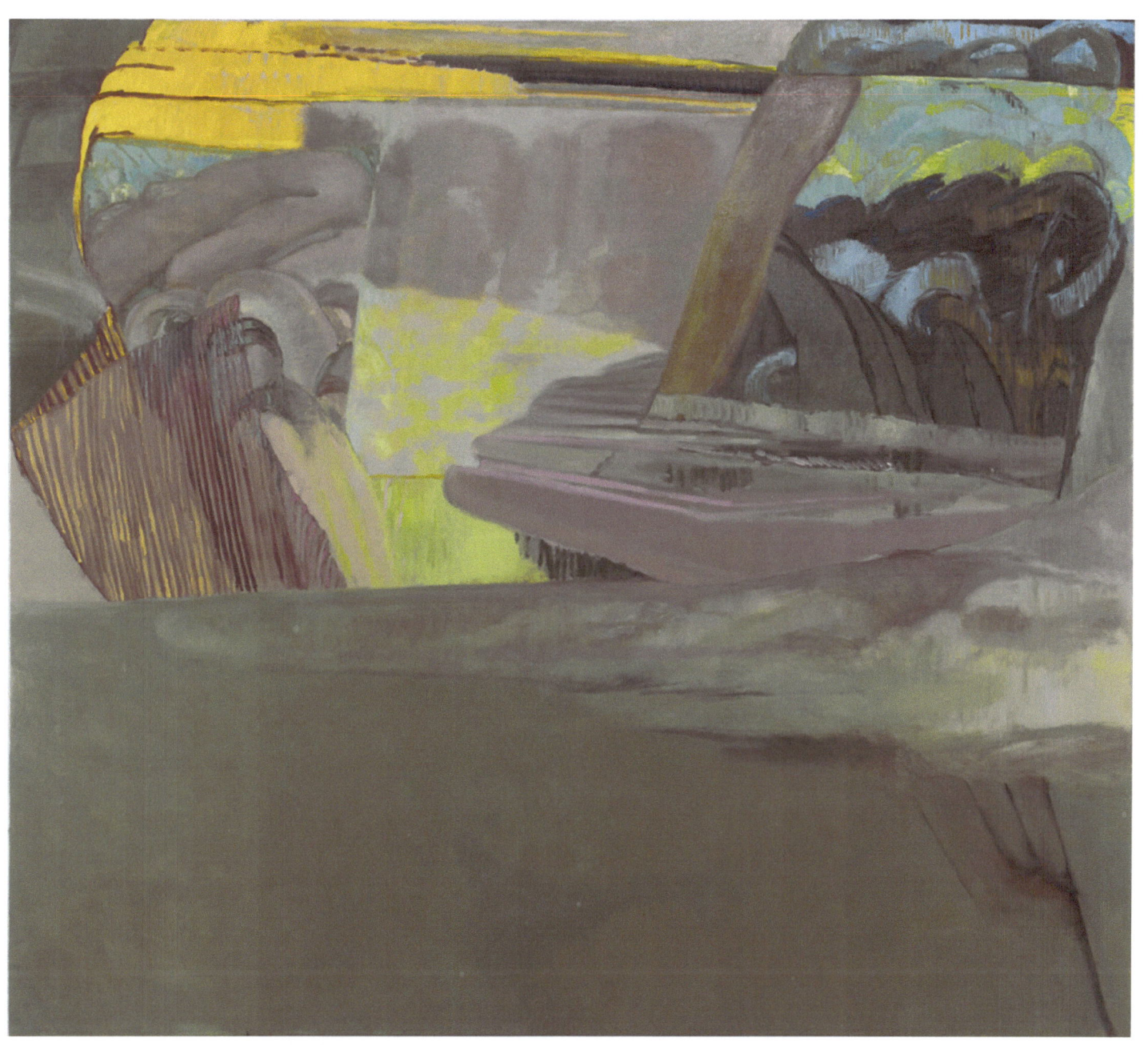

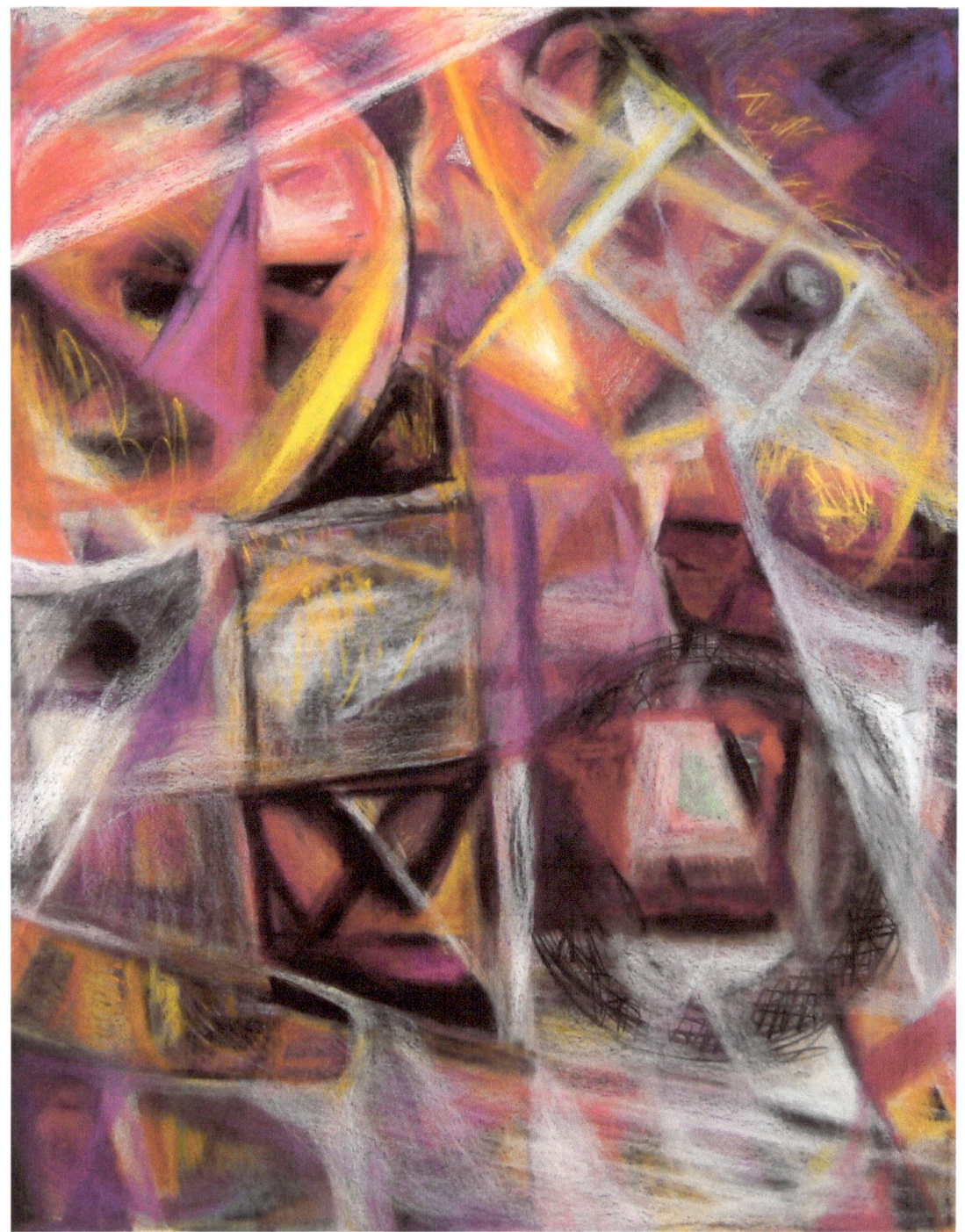

barr, m g

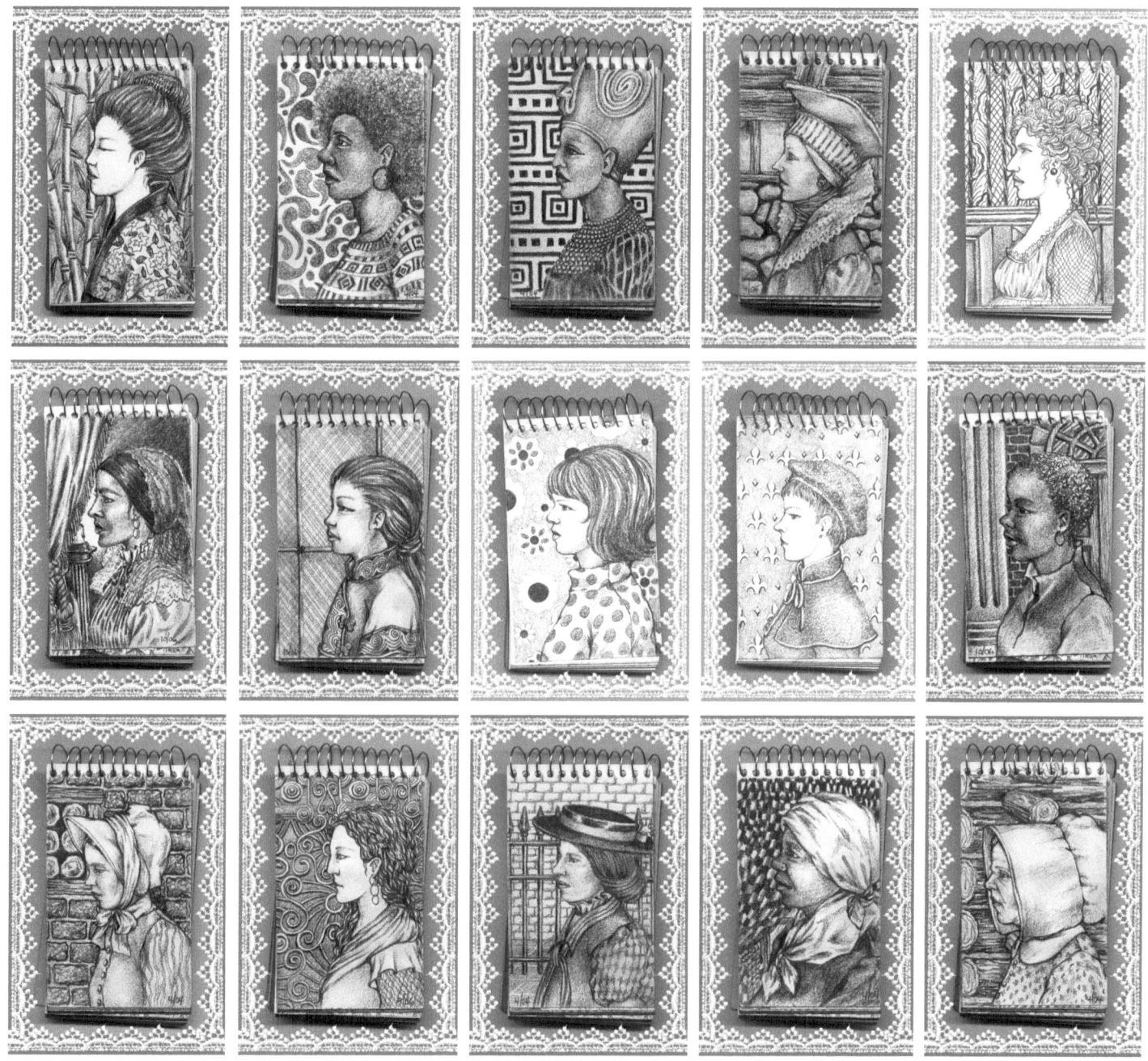

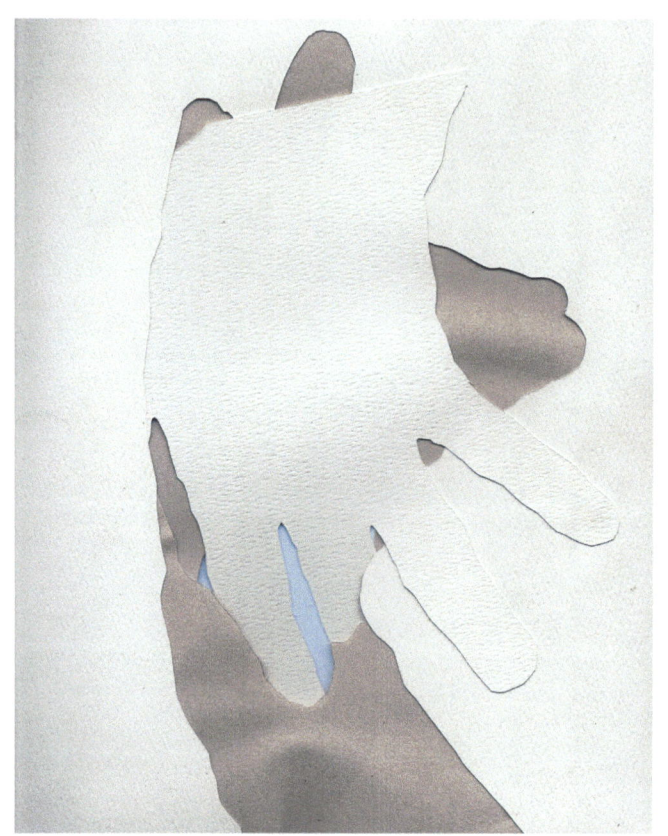 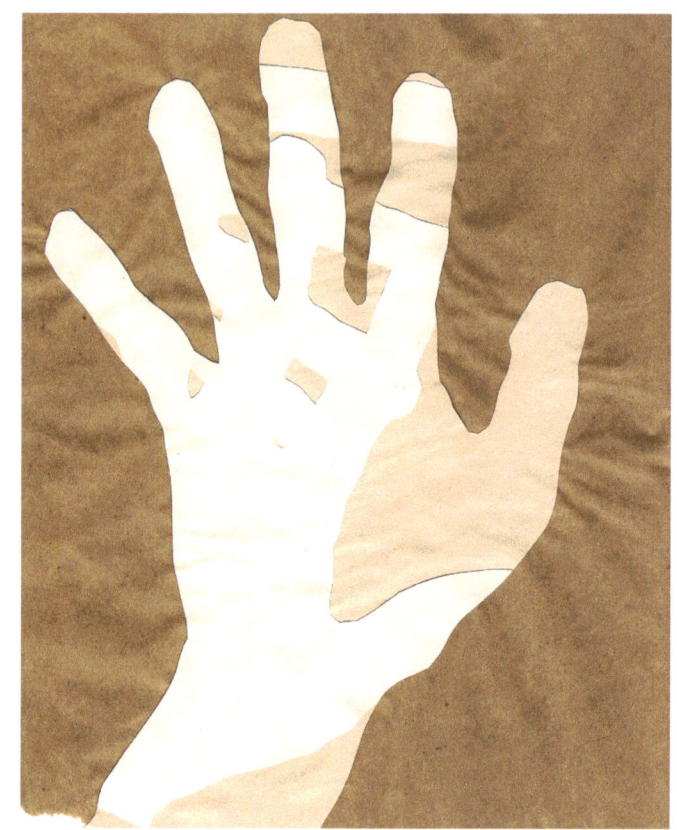

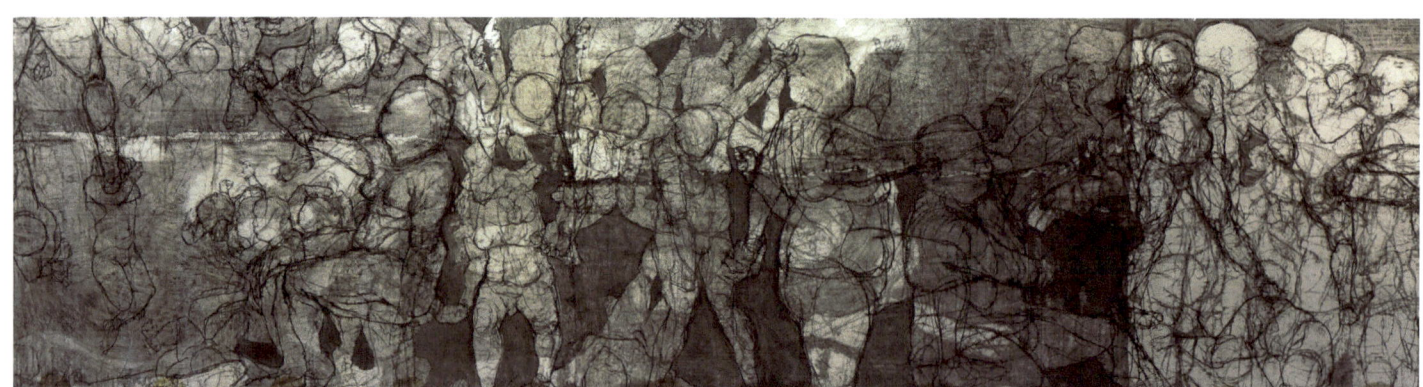

moore, maurice

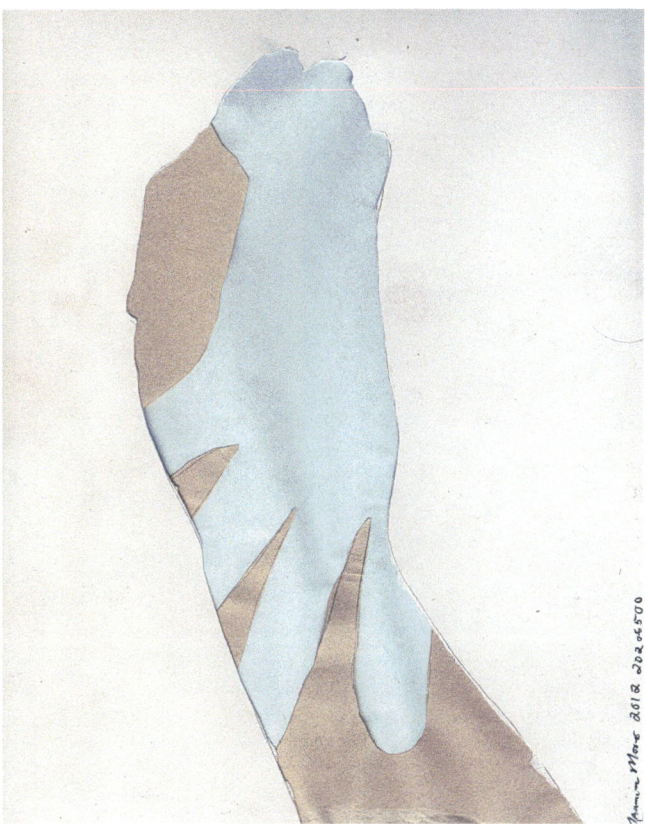

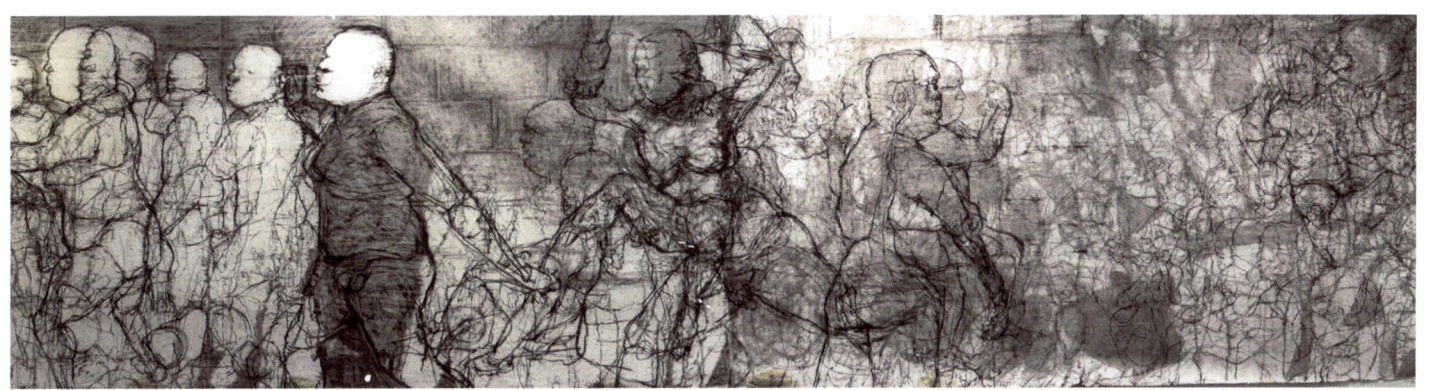

moore, maurice

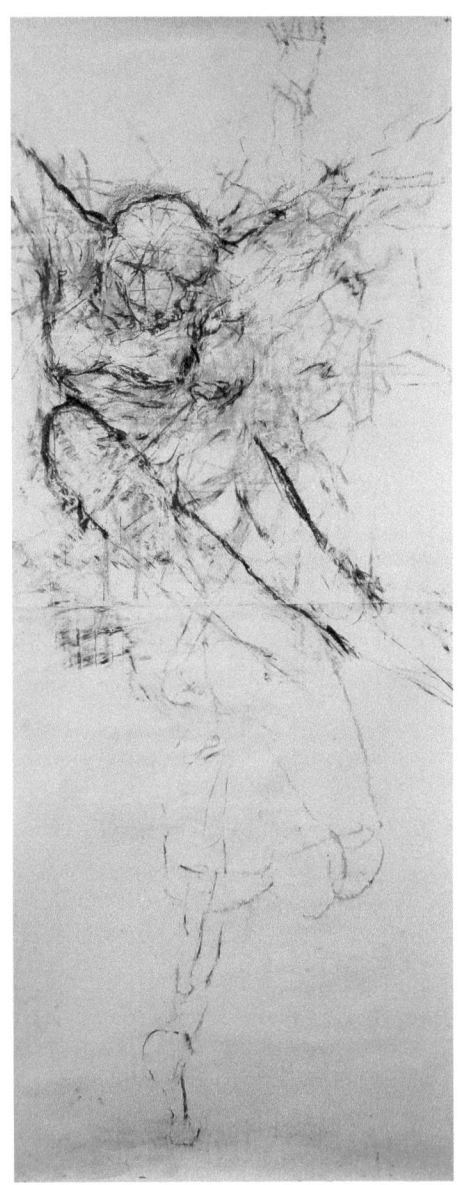 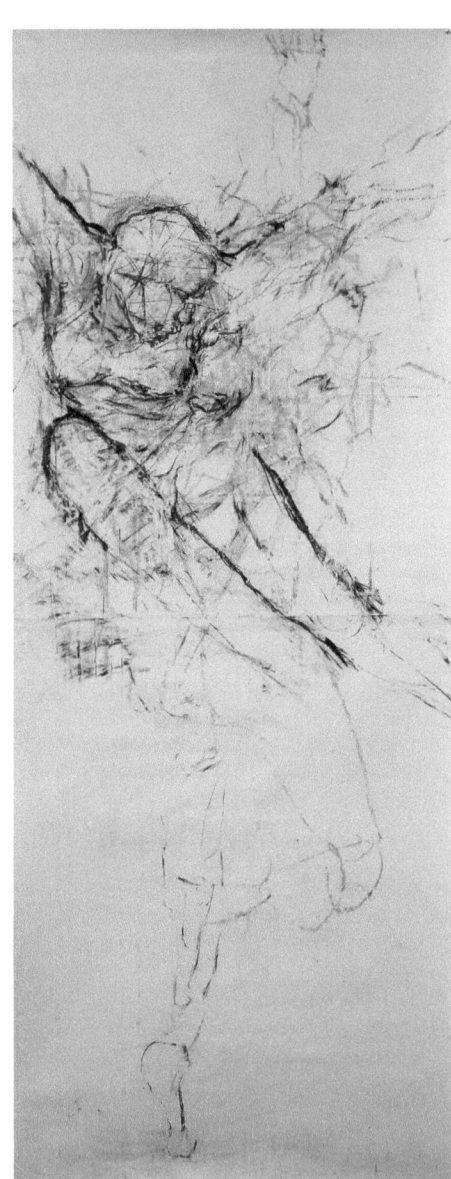 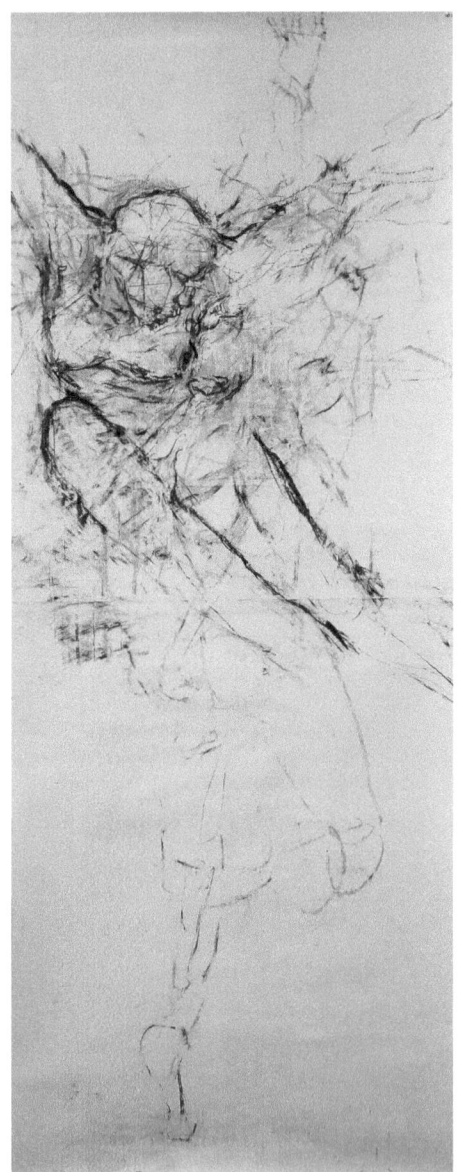

moore, maurice

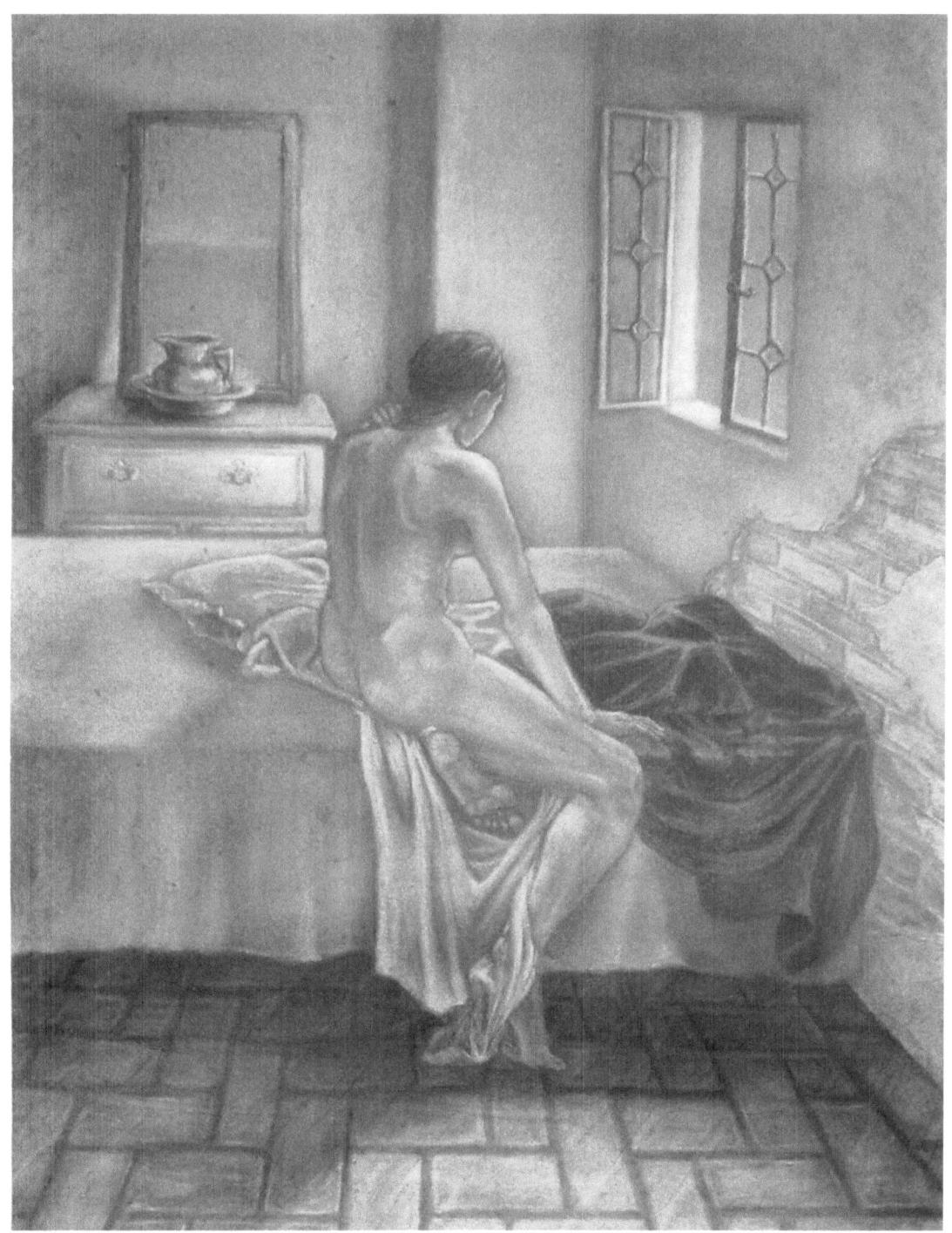

tisdell, suzanne

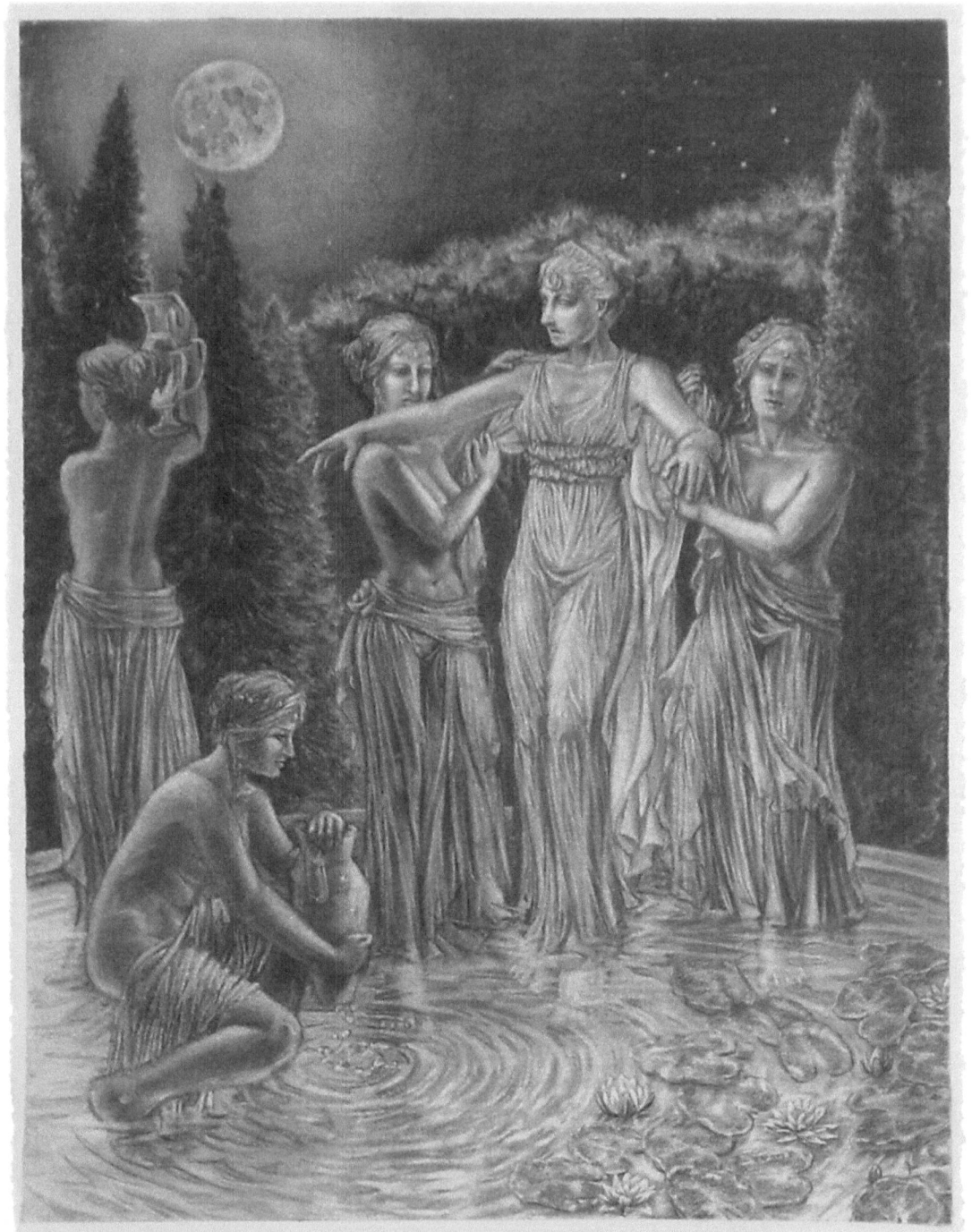

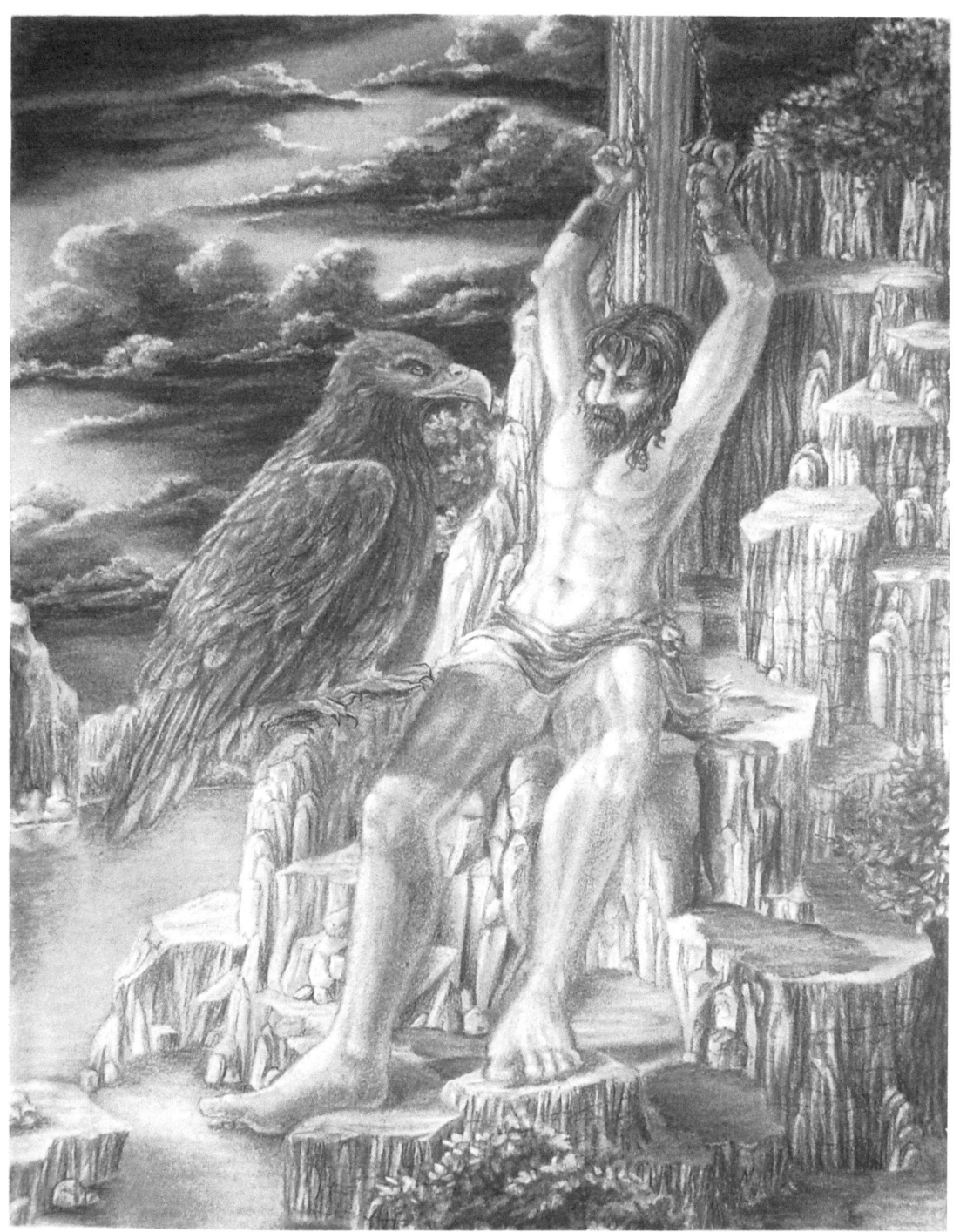

tisdell, suzanne

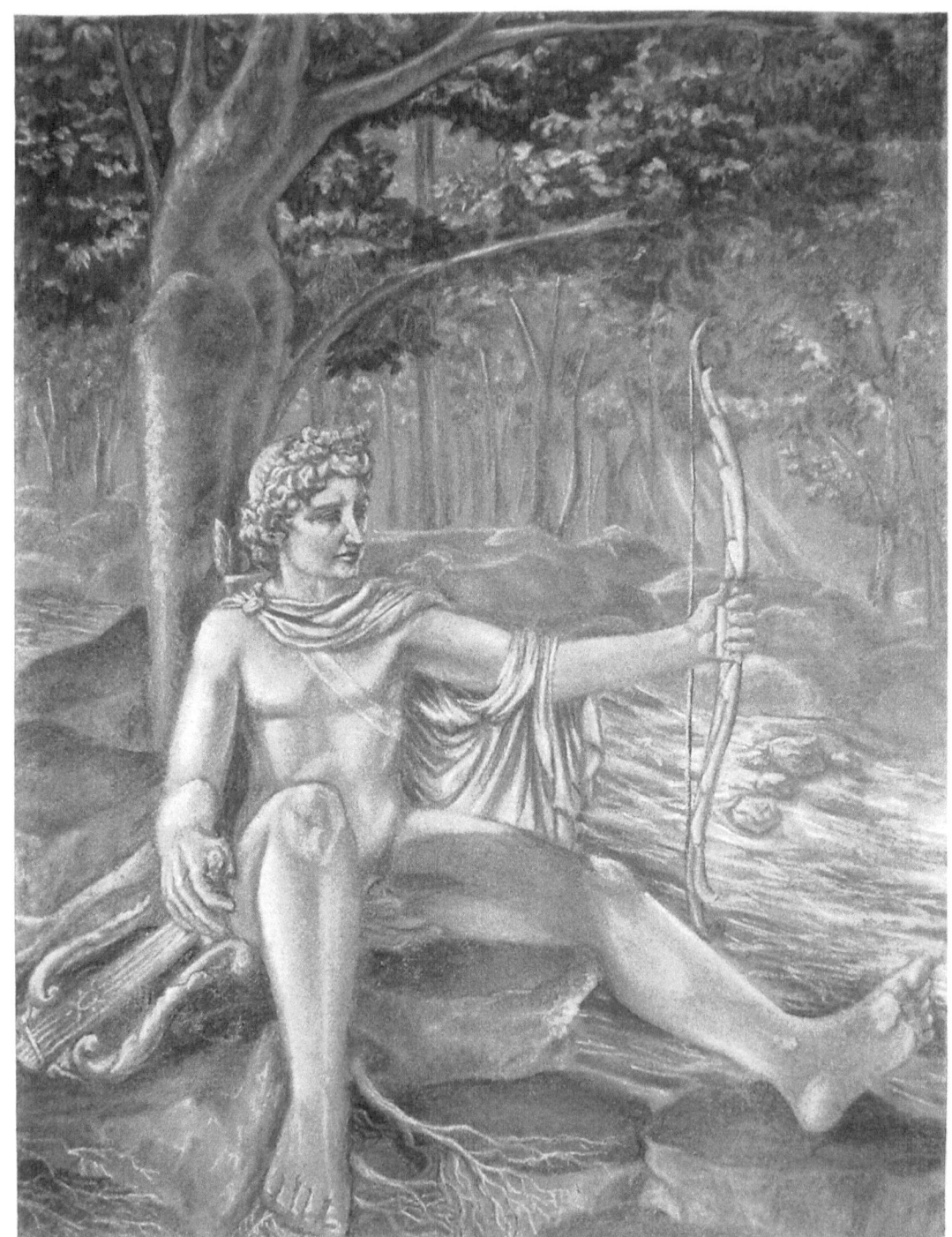

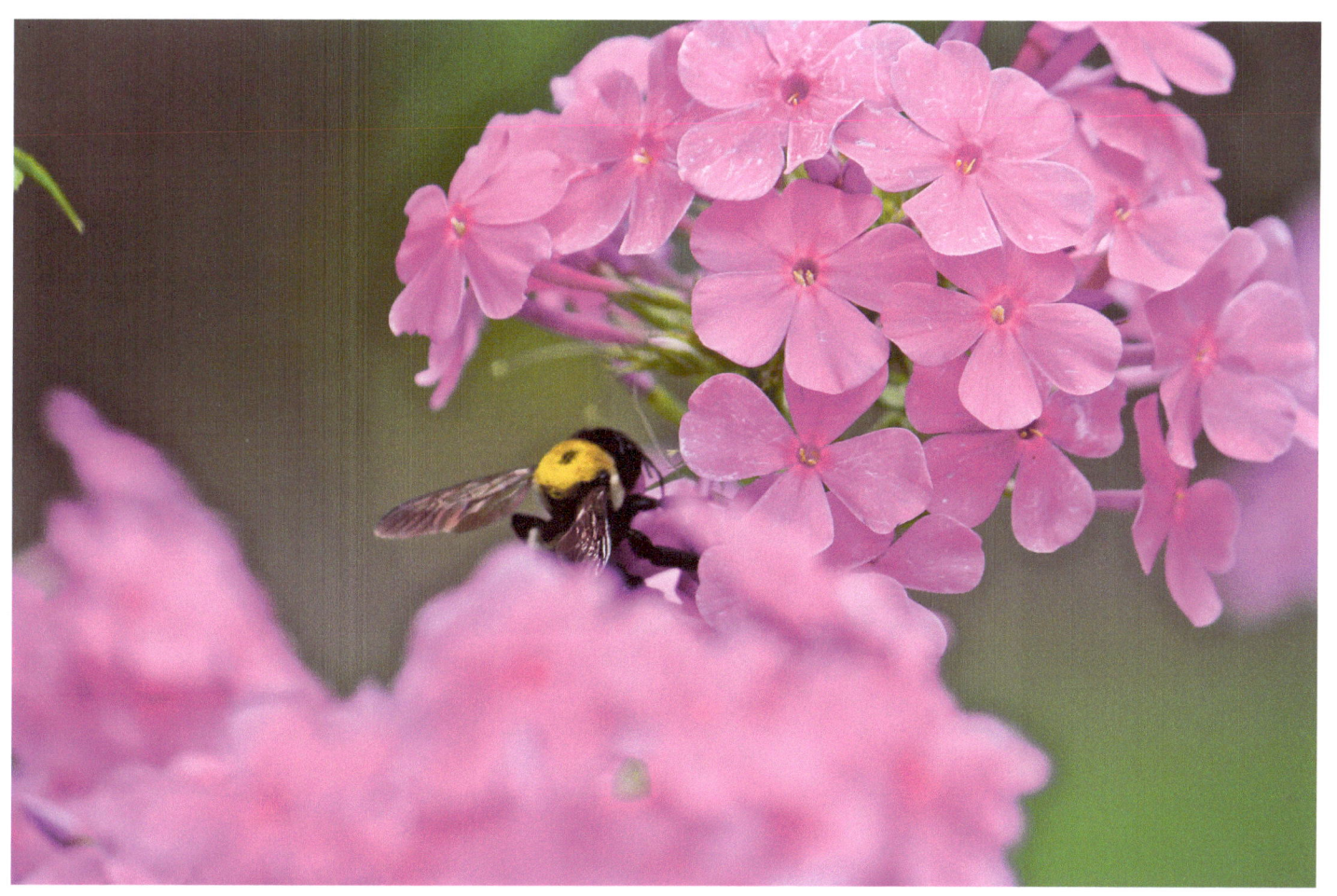

robinson, miranda

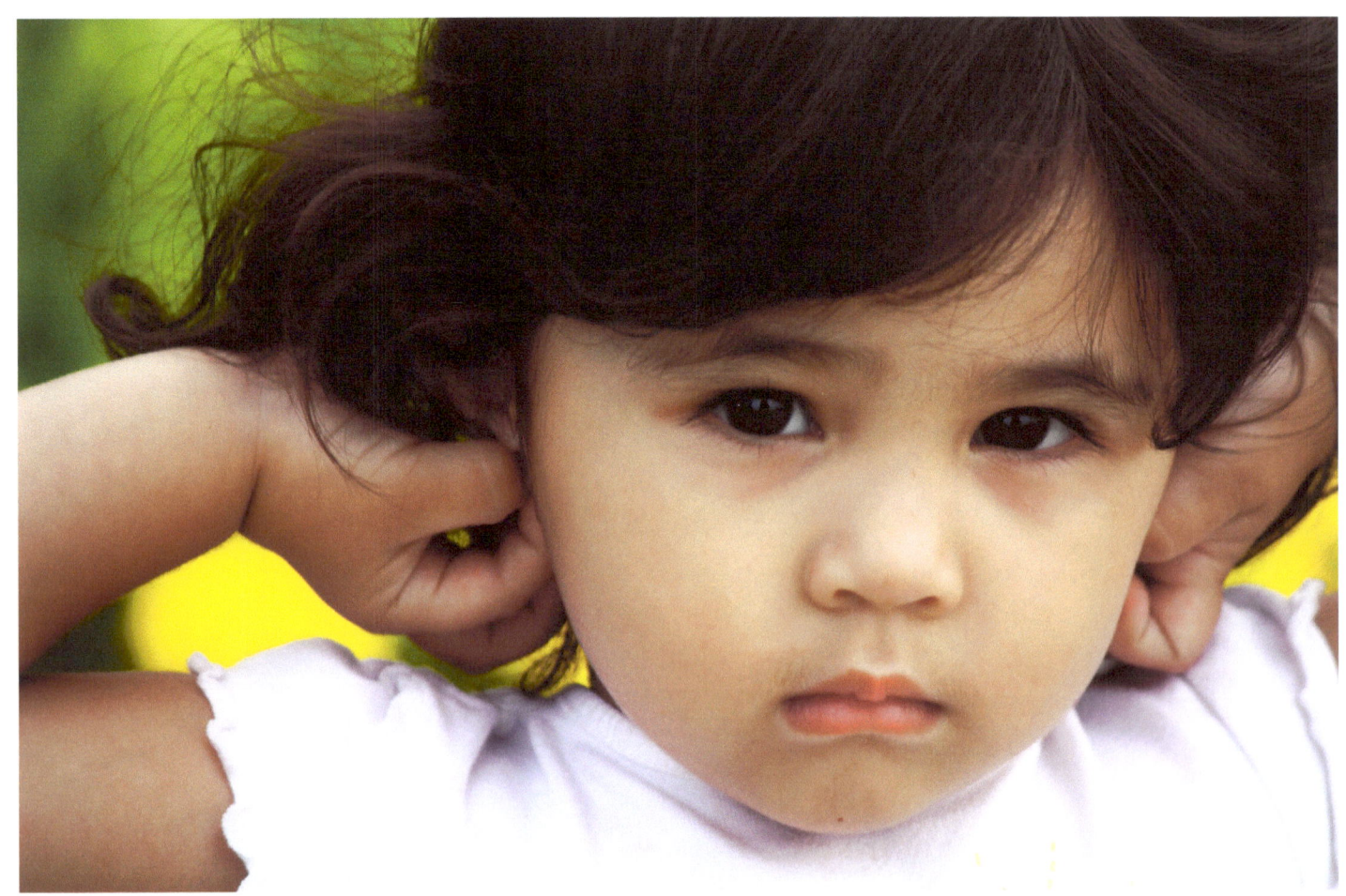

robinson, miranda

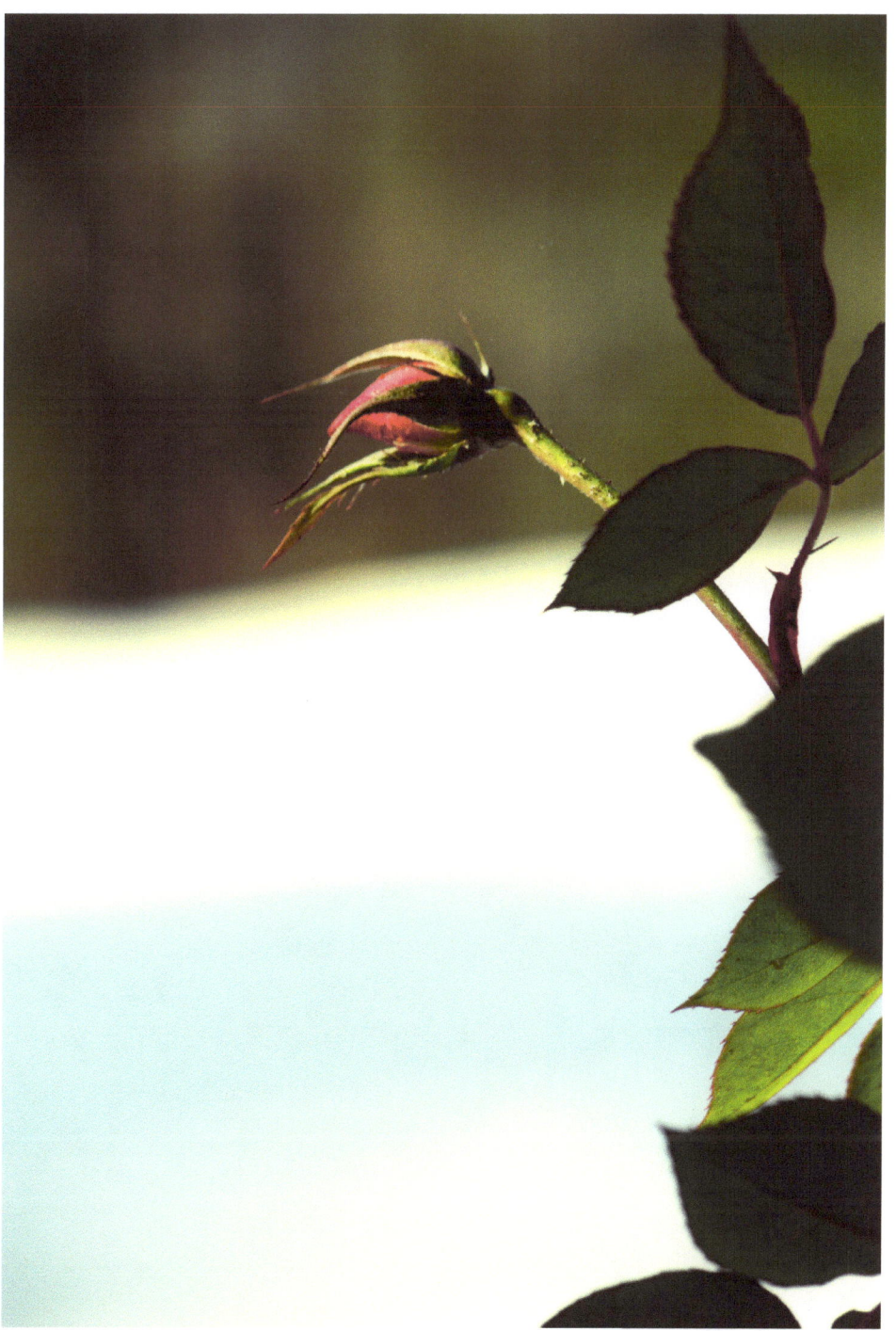

robinson, miranda

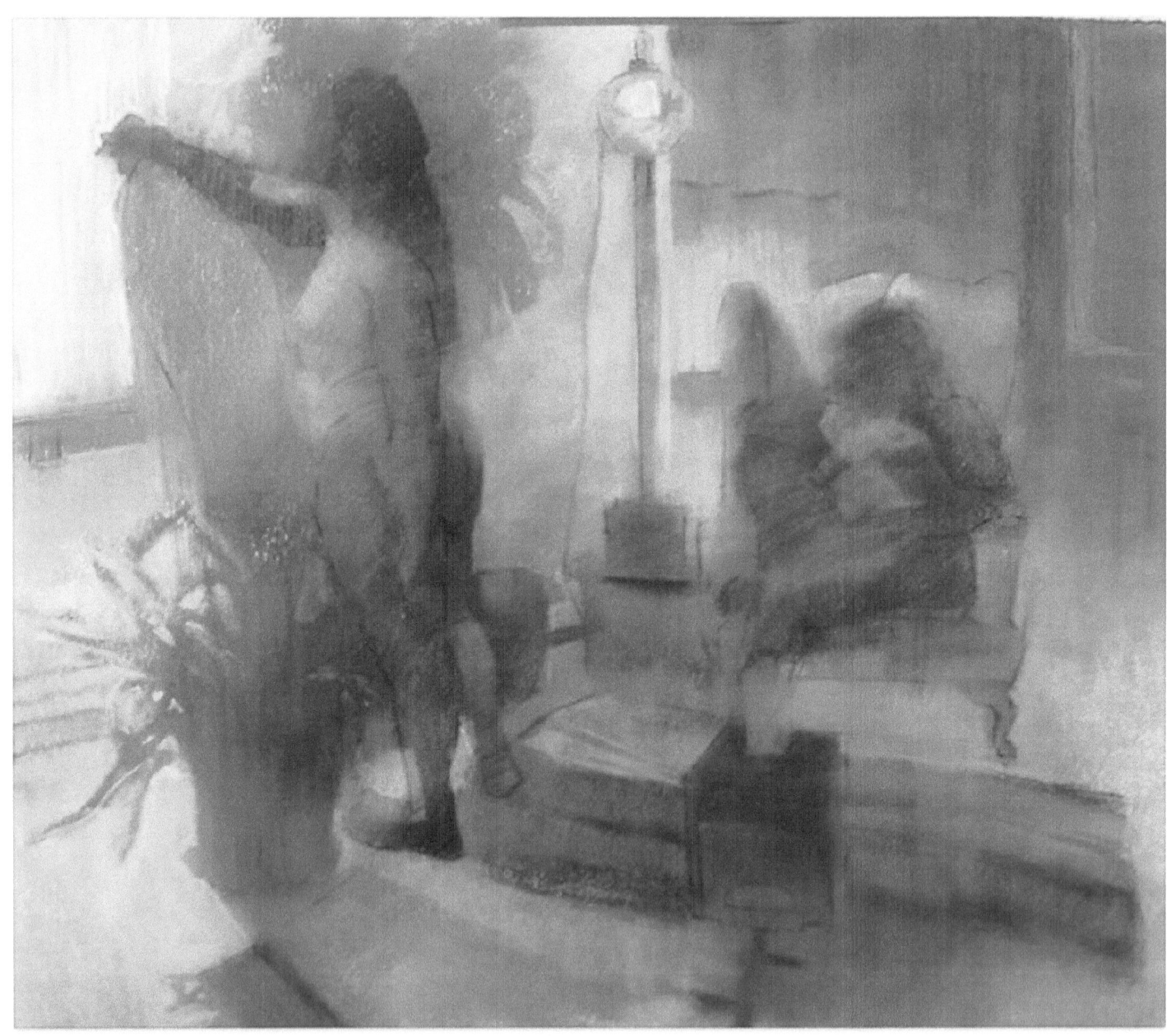

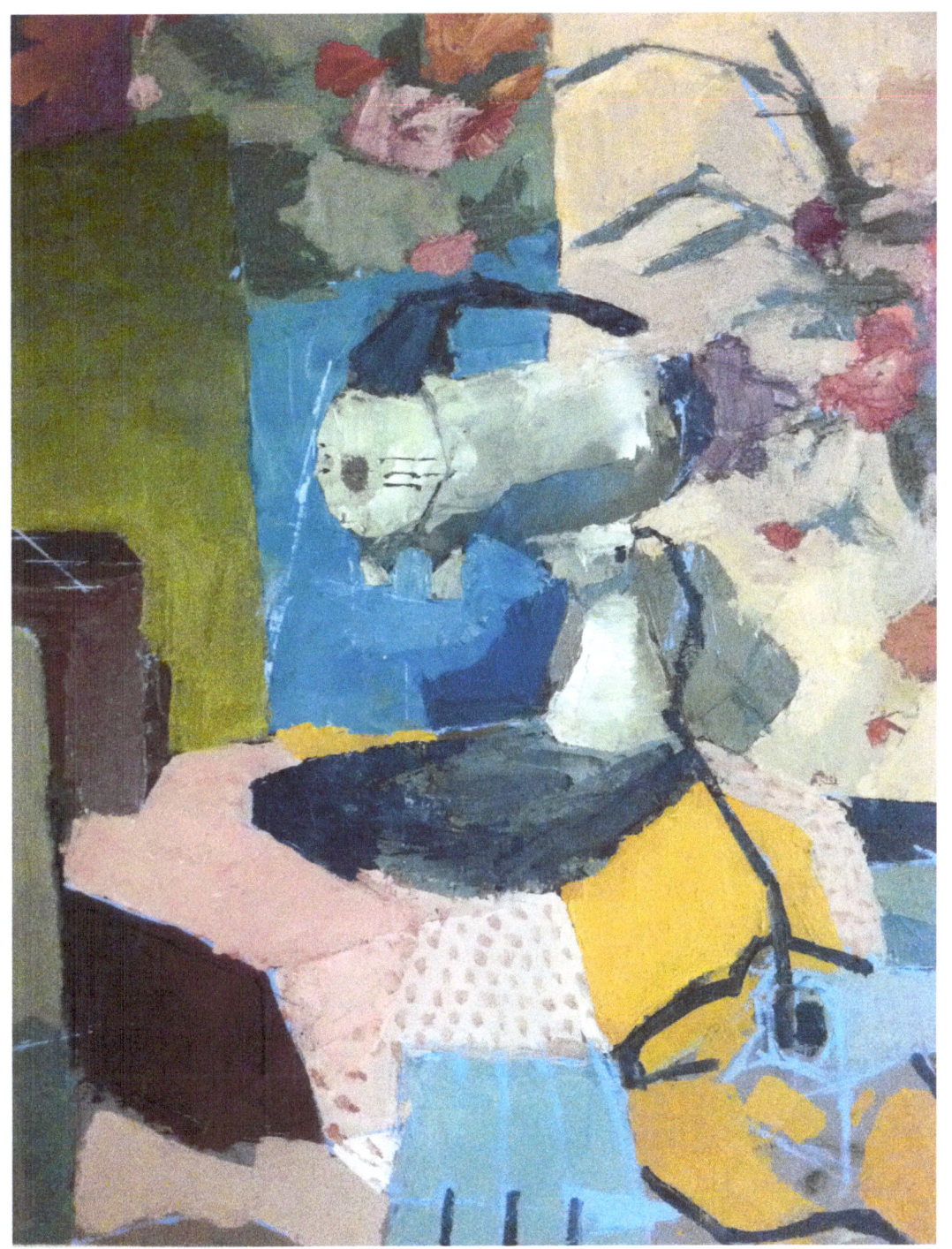

shipman, bennett

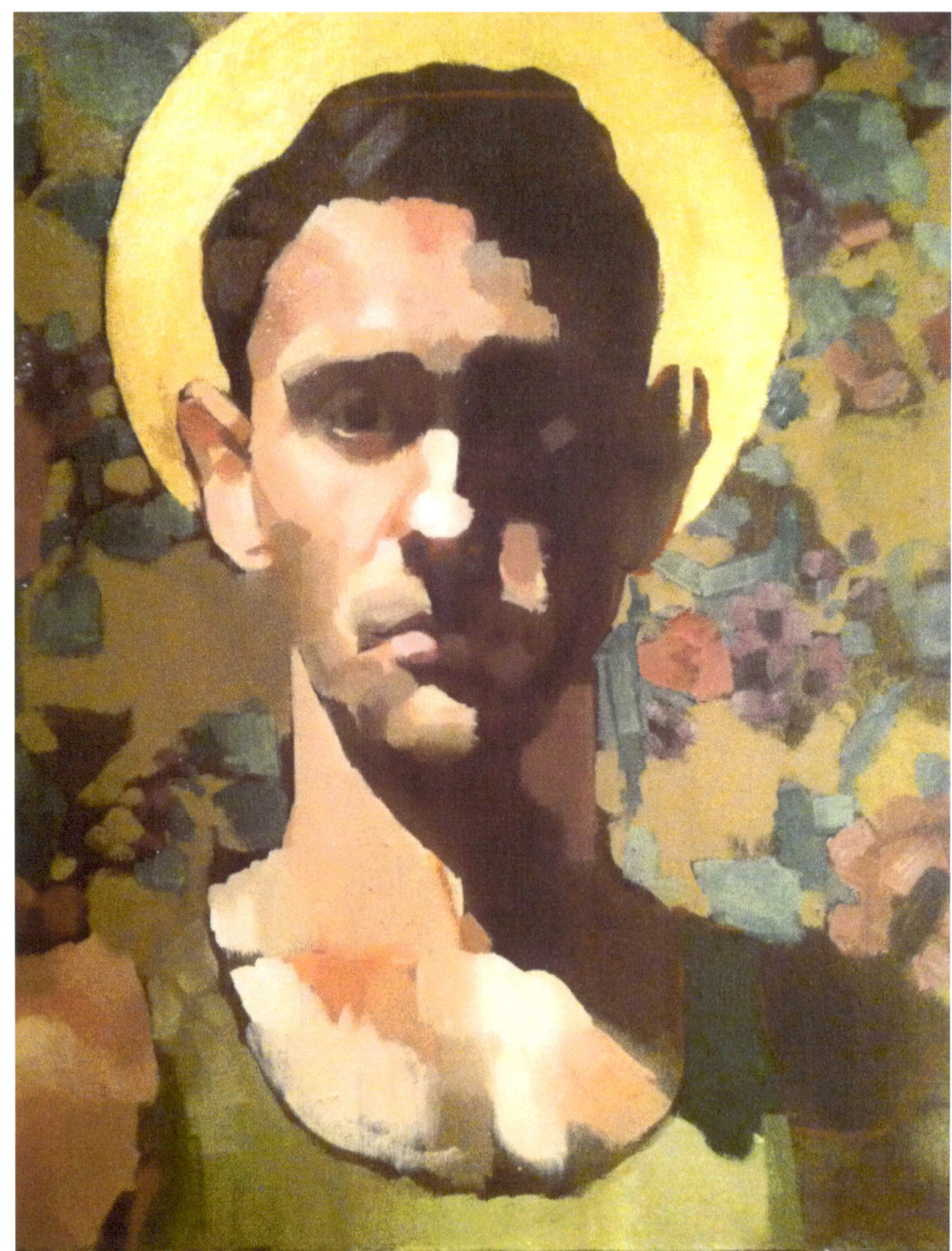

shipman, bennett

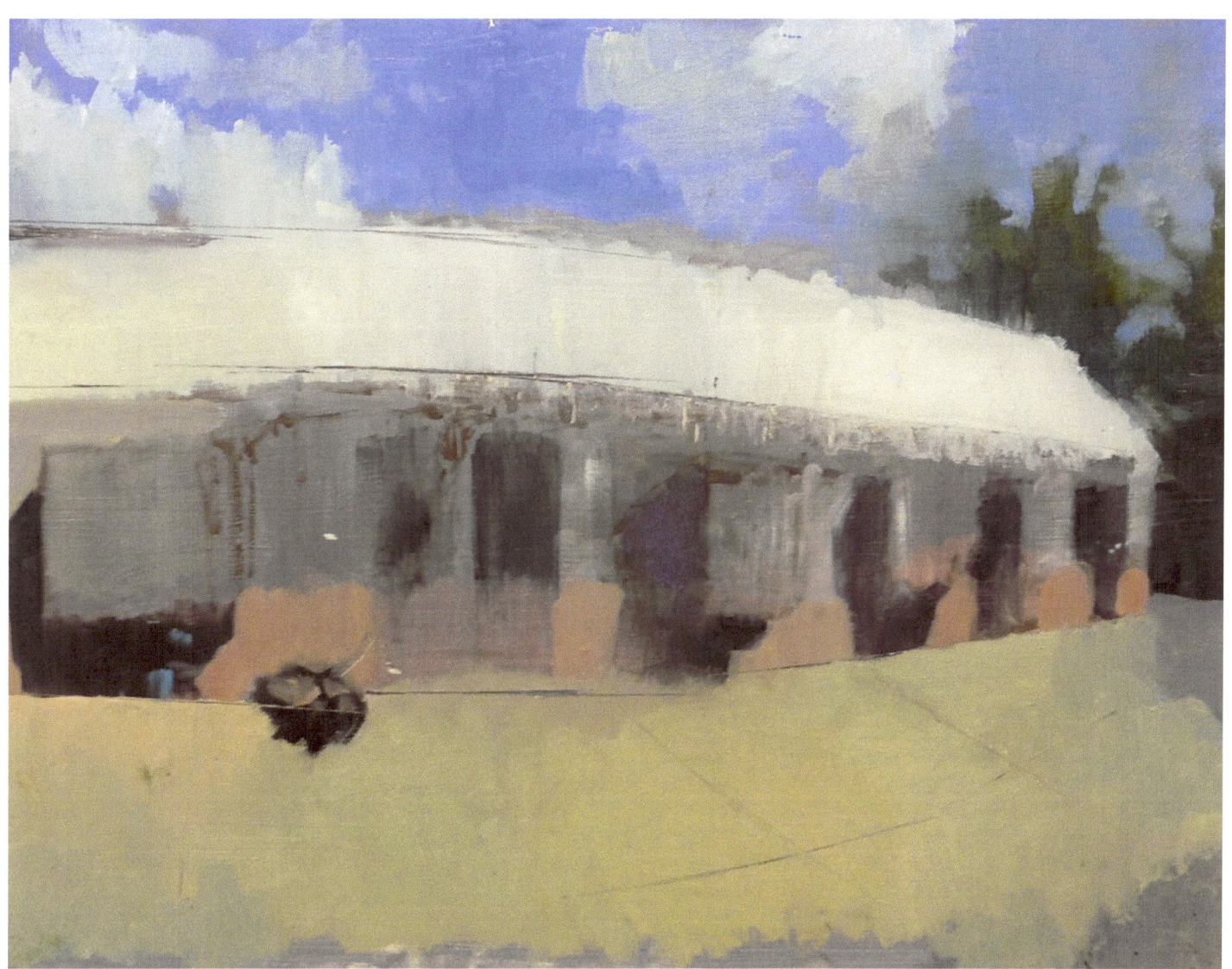

shipman, bennett

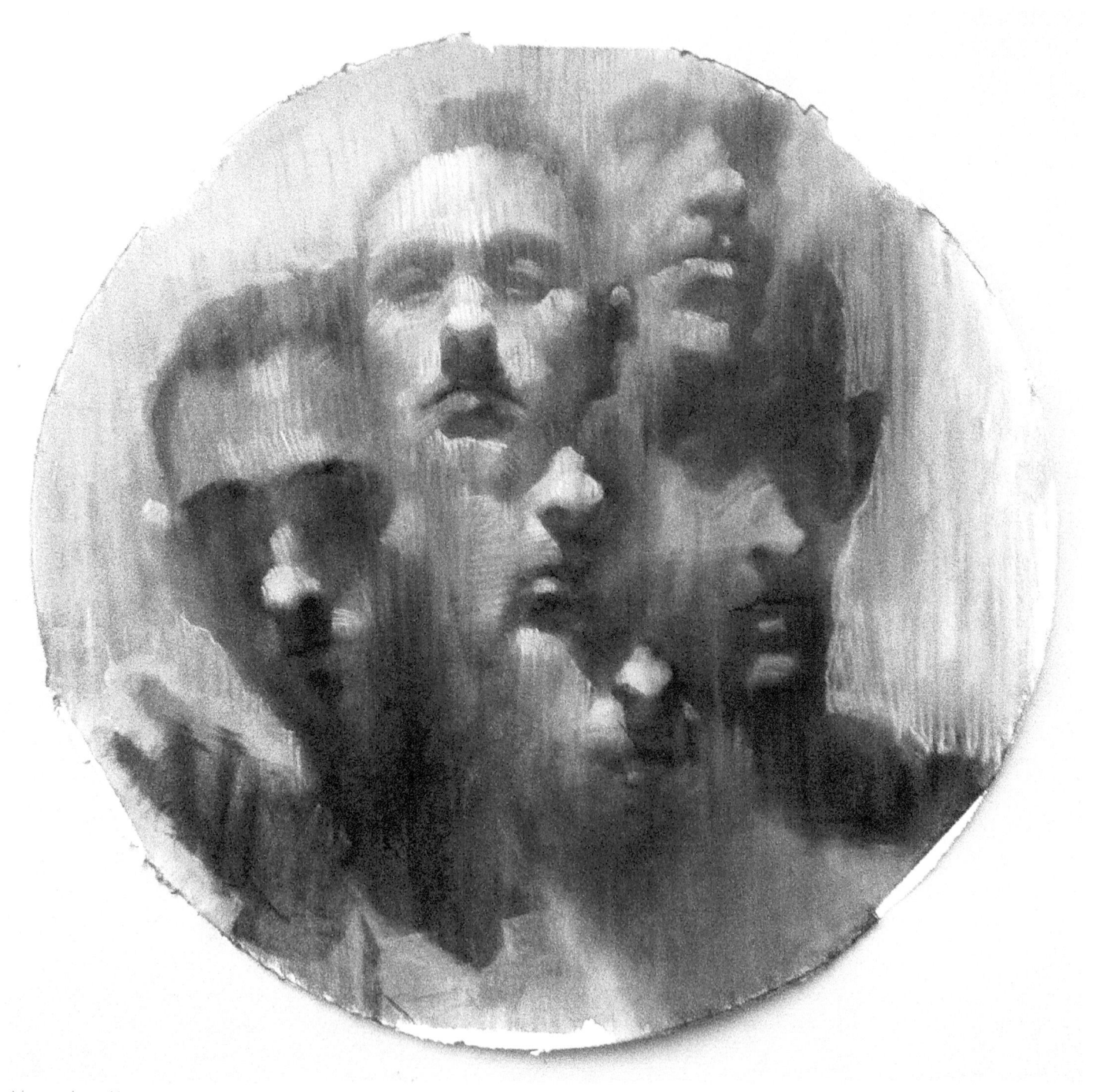

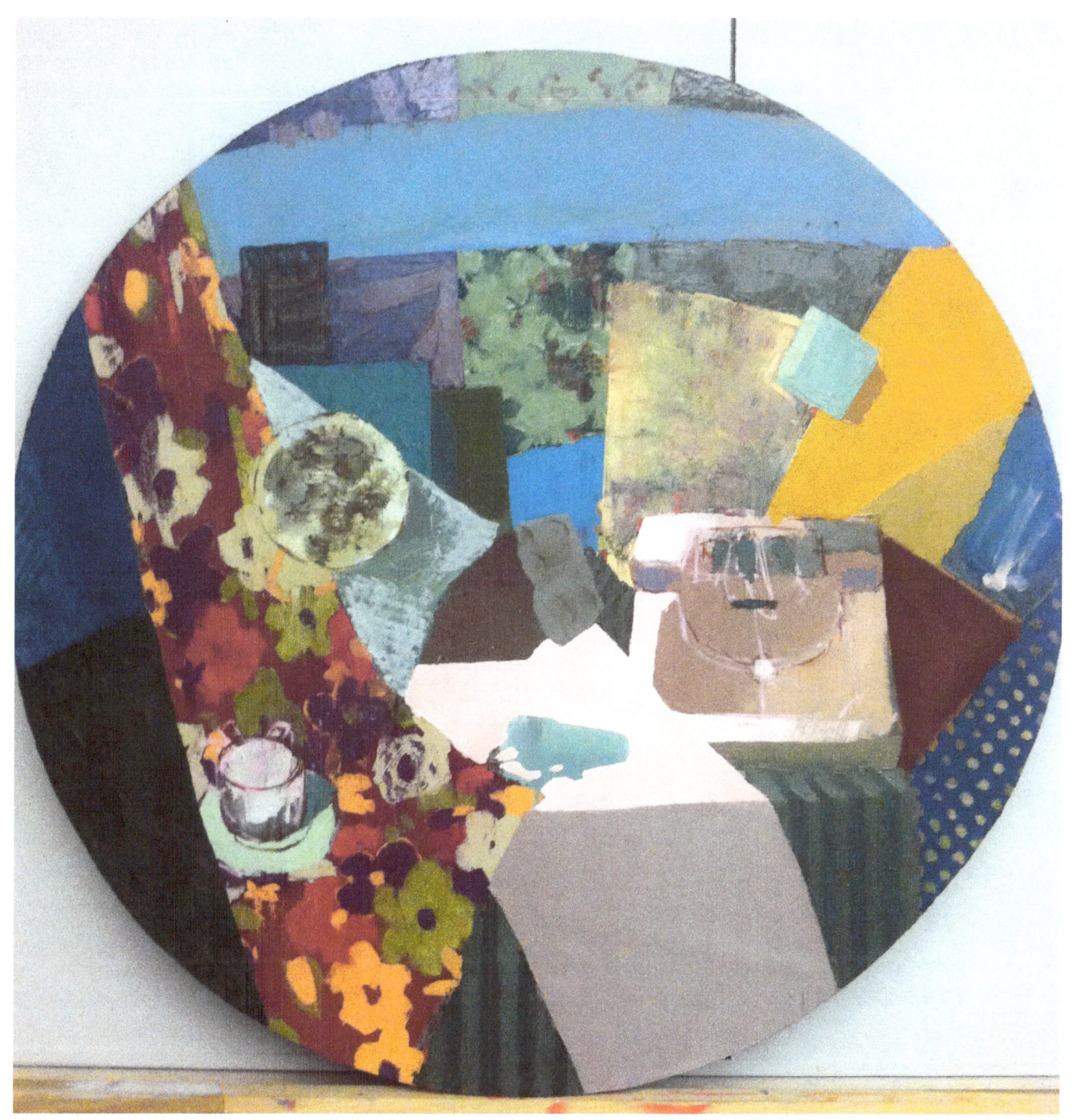

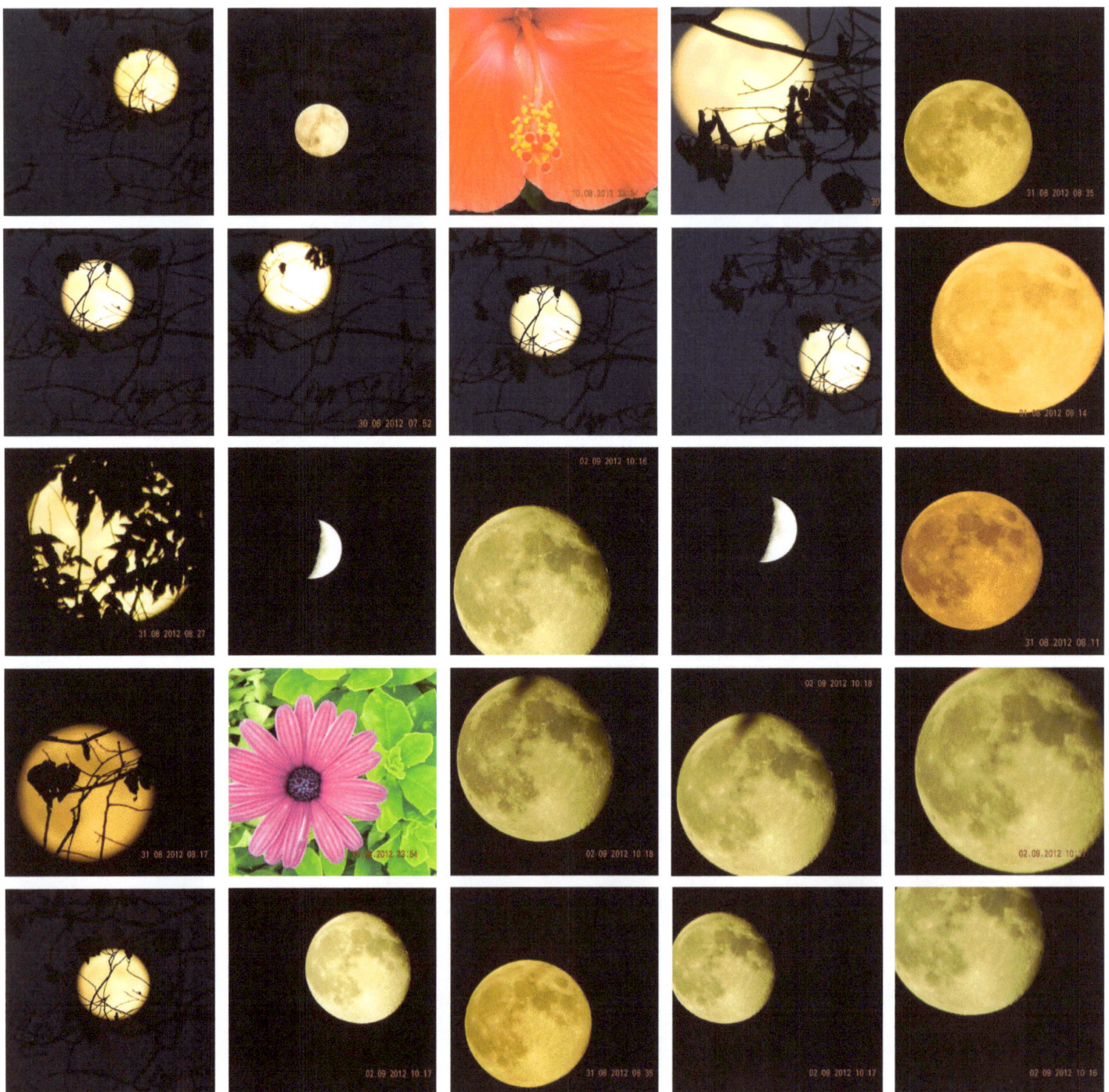

belluardo, s a

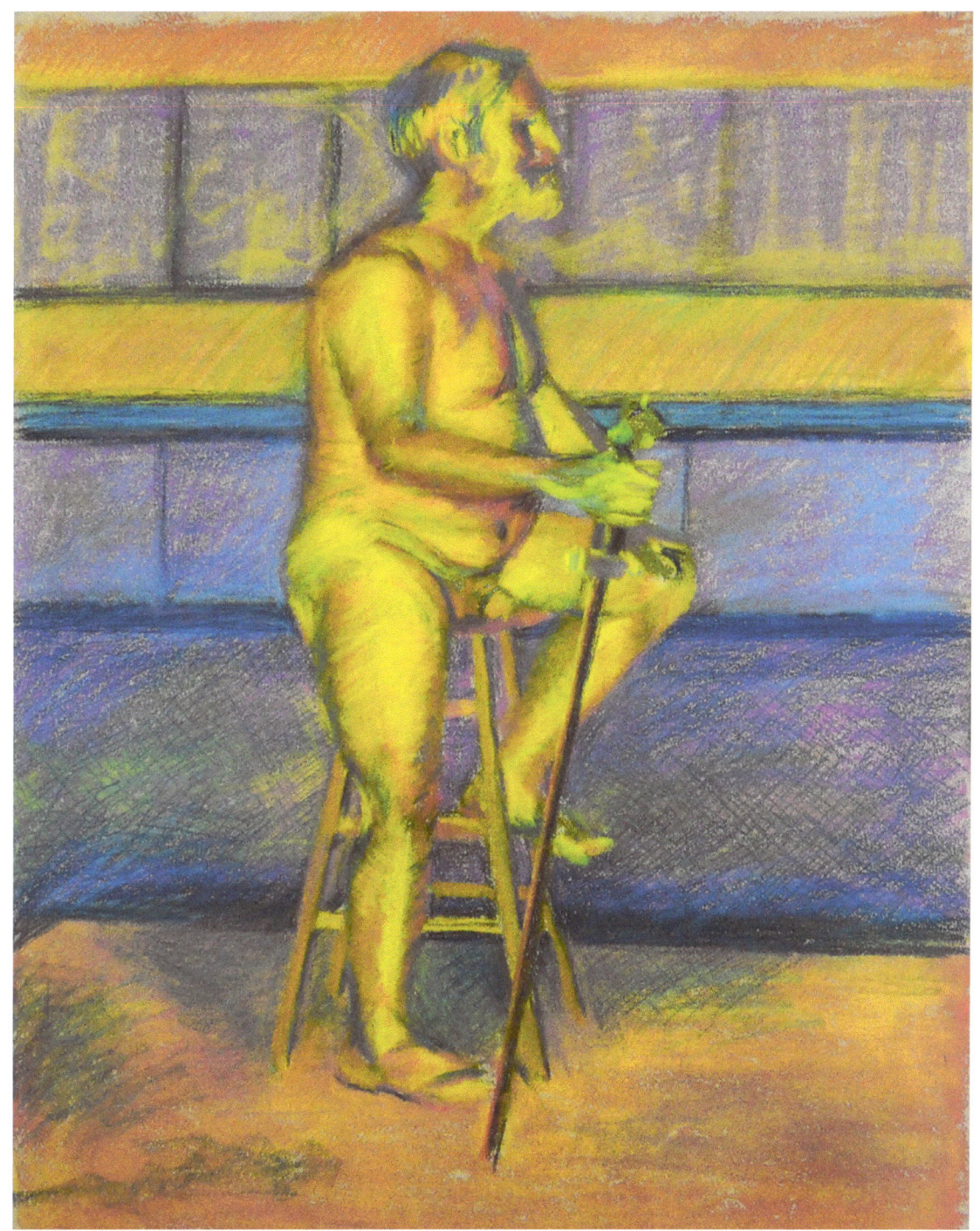

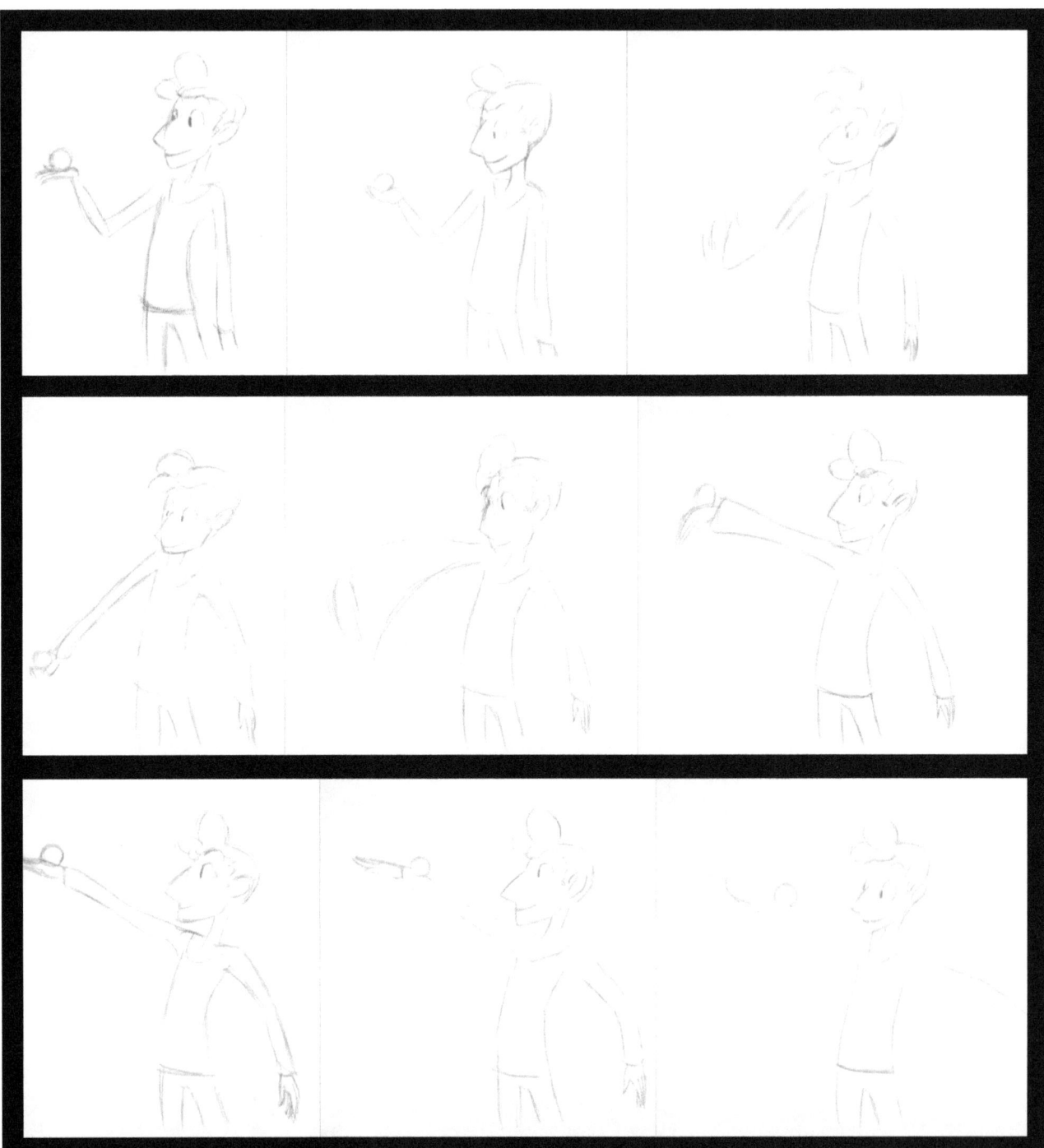

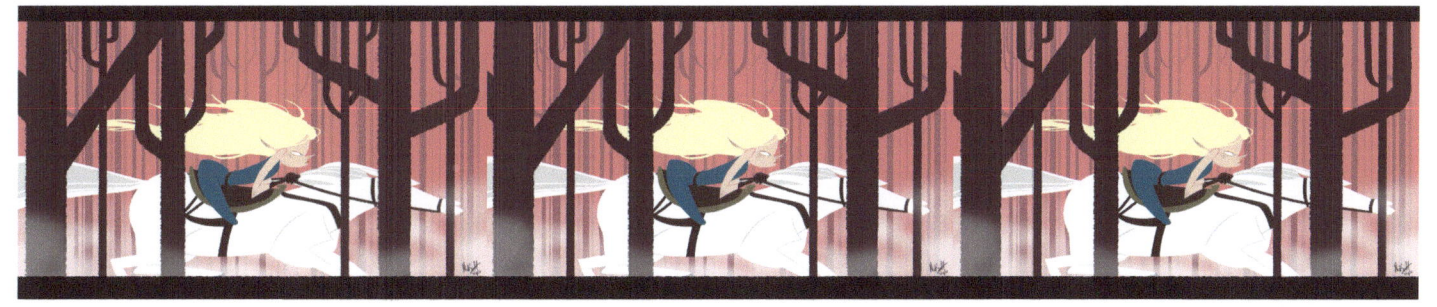

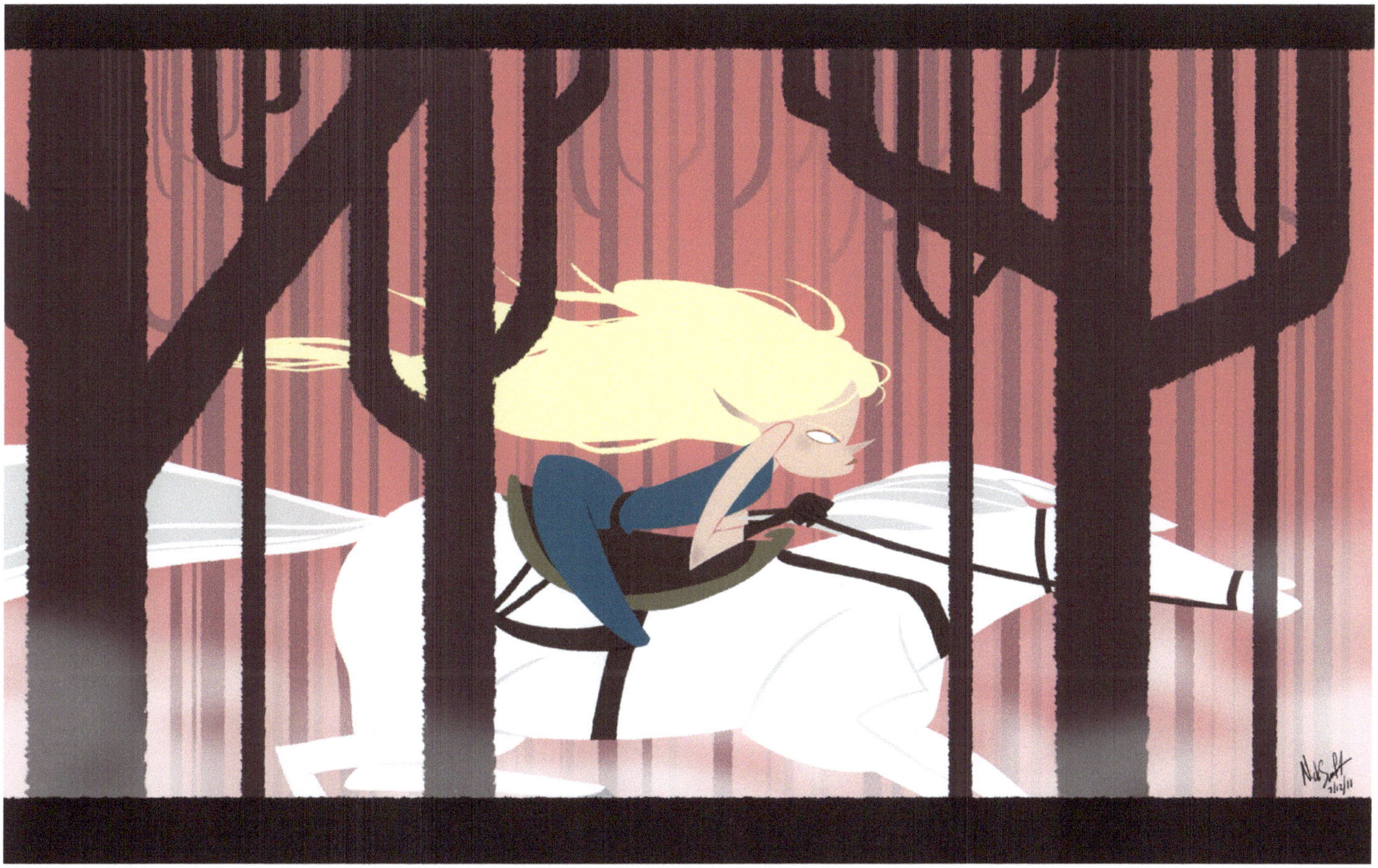

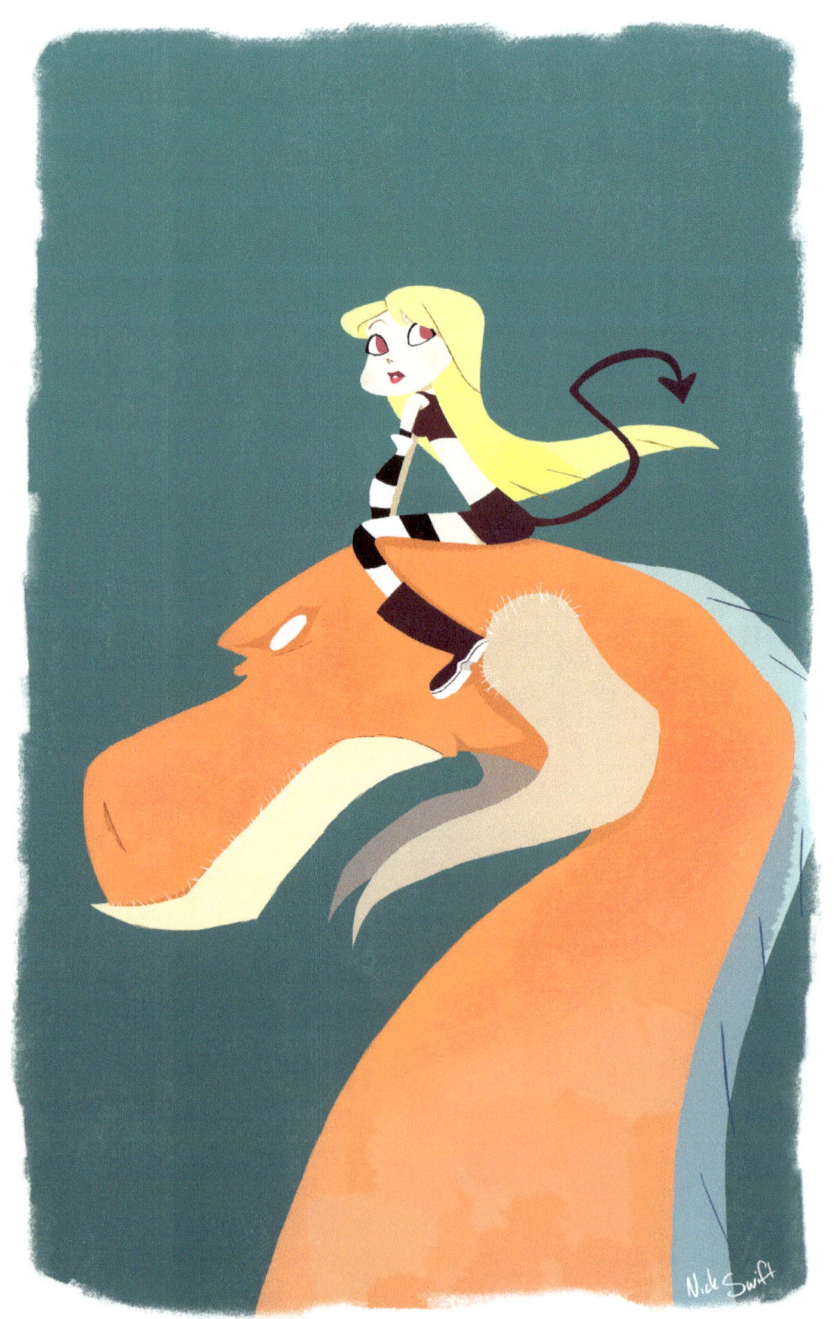

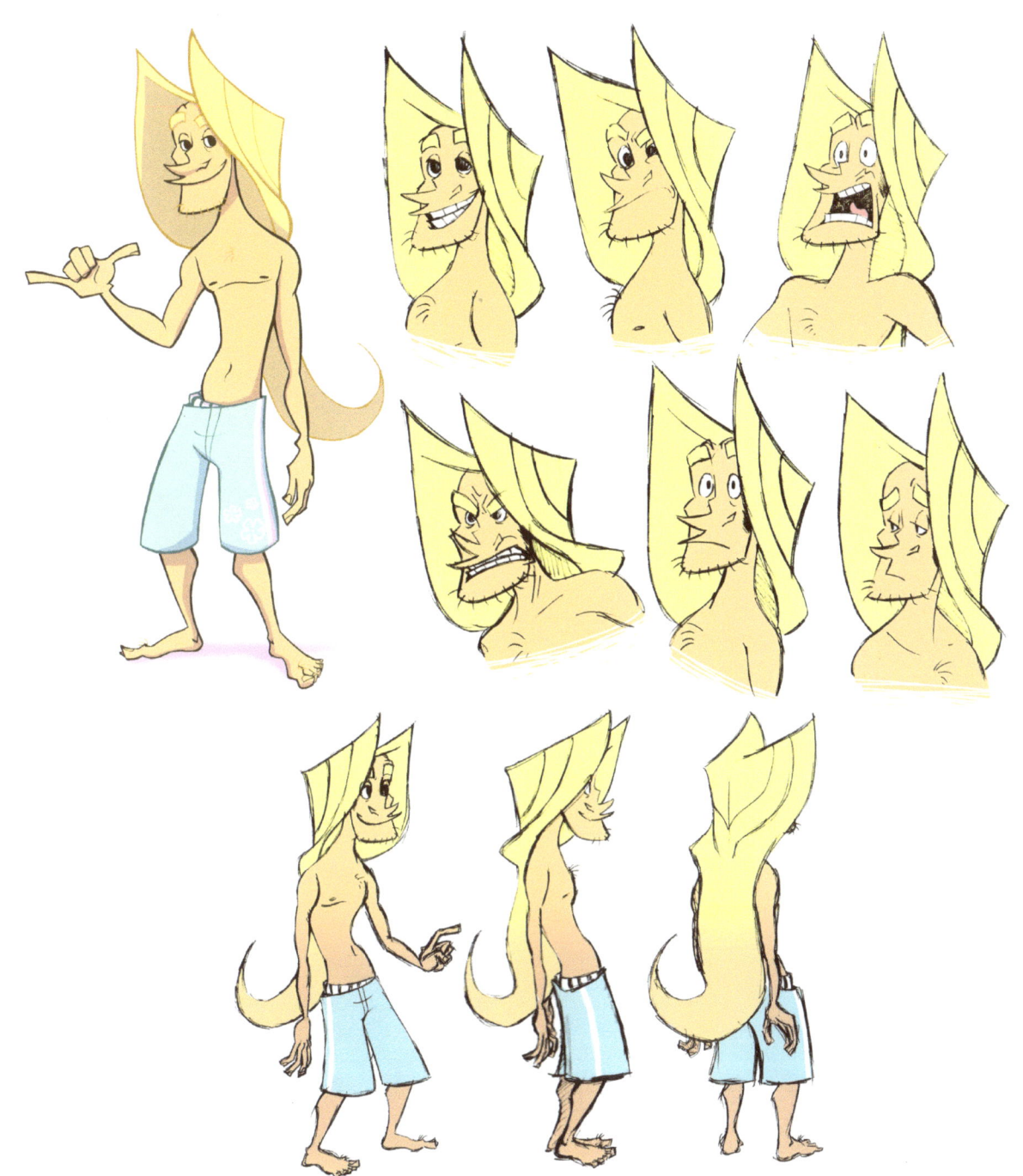

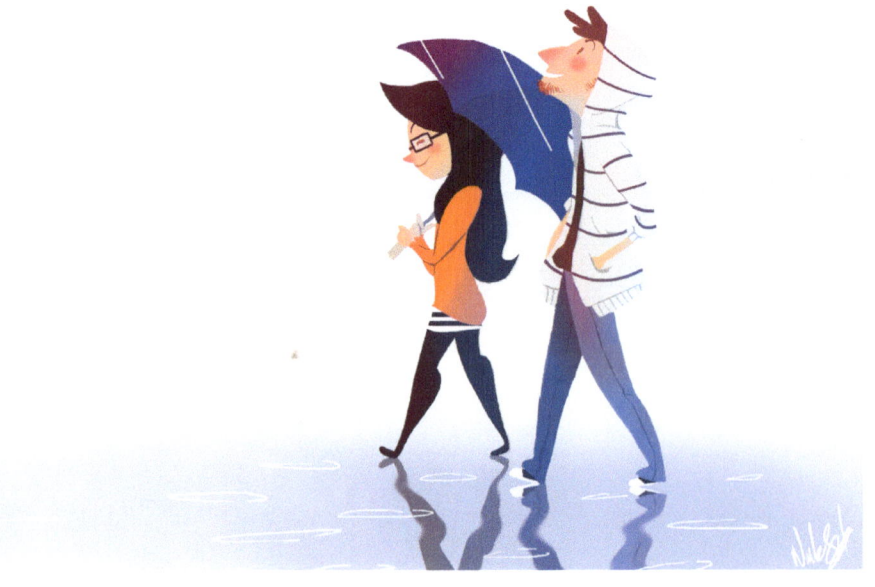

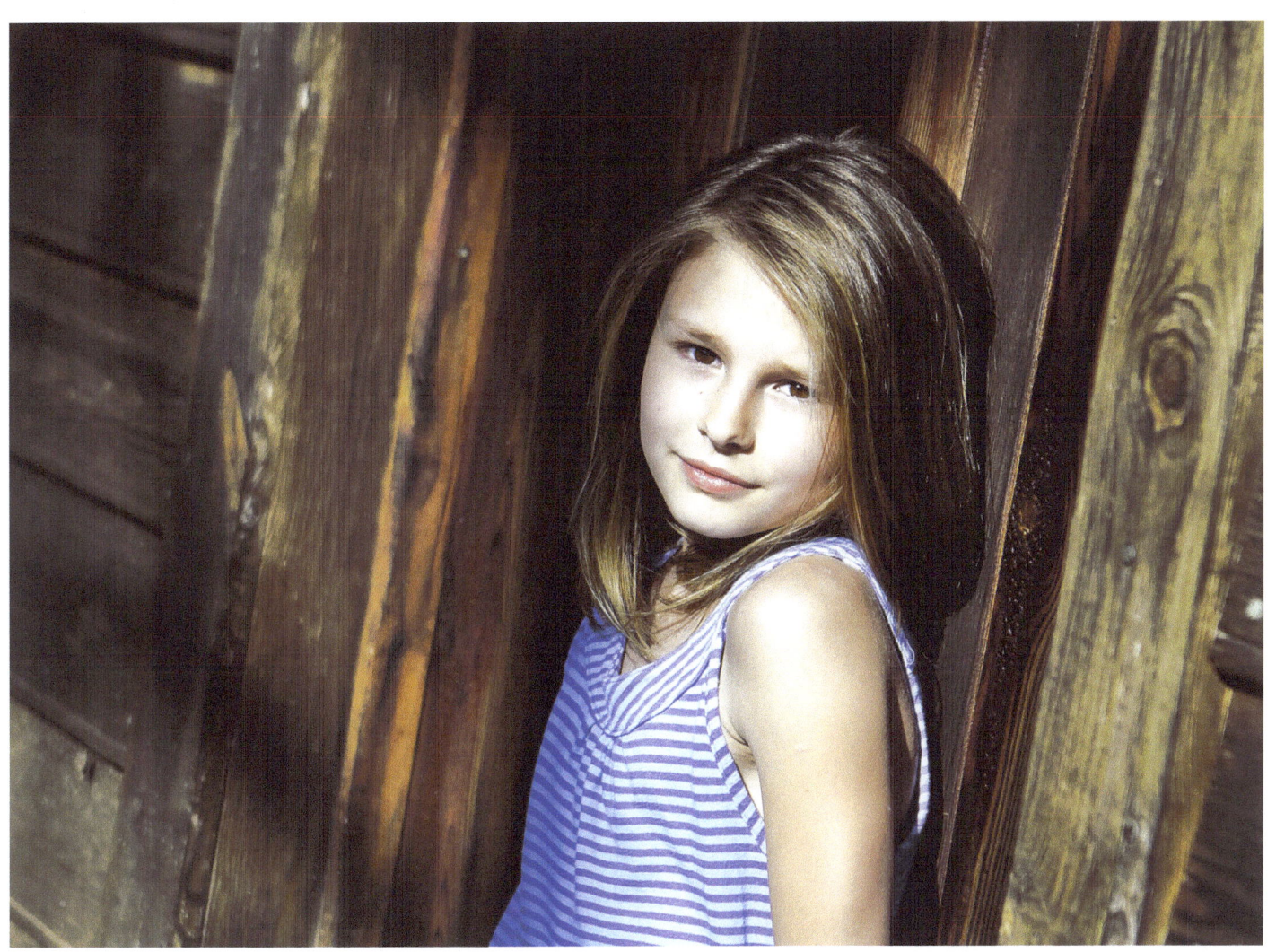

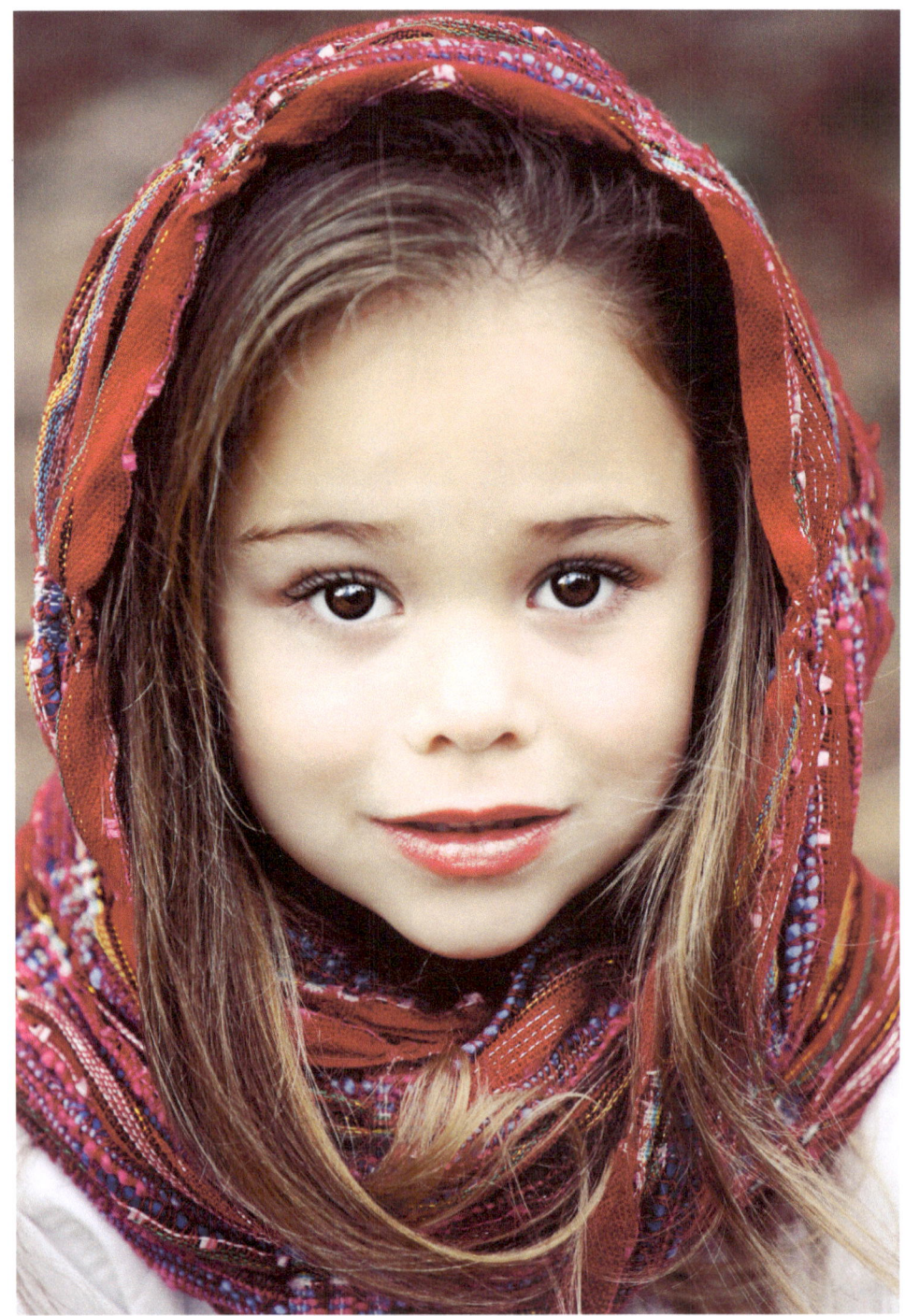

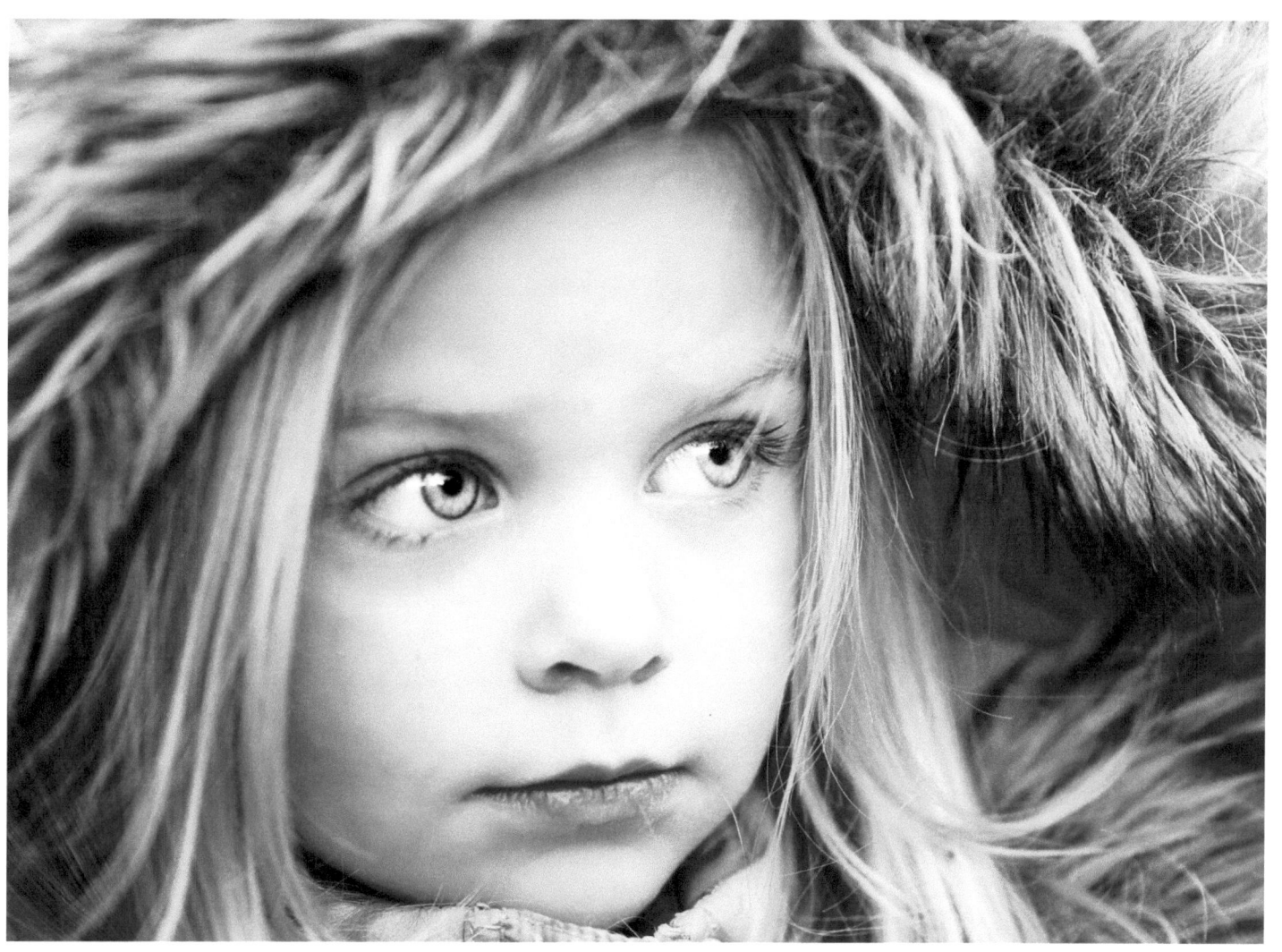

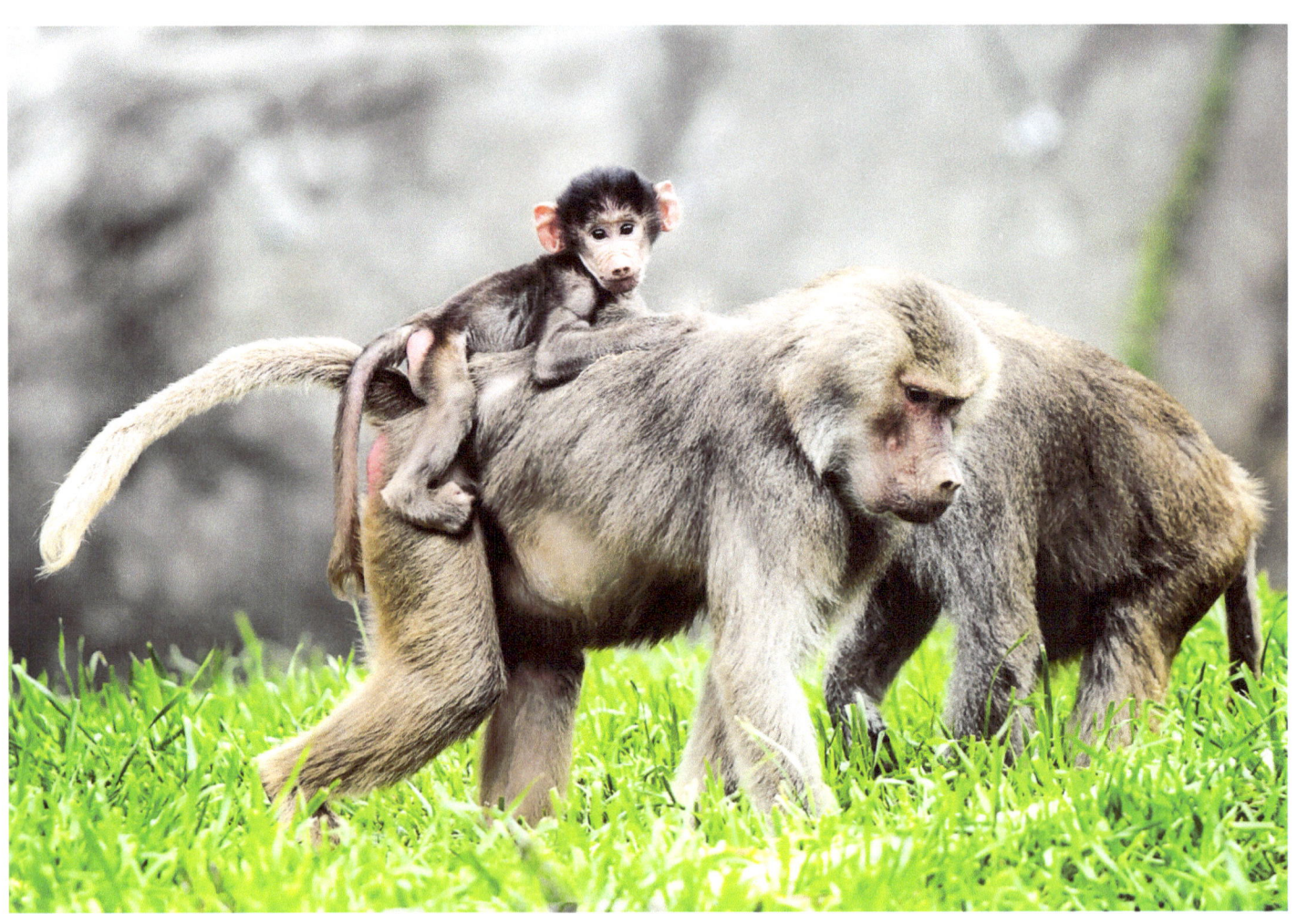

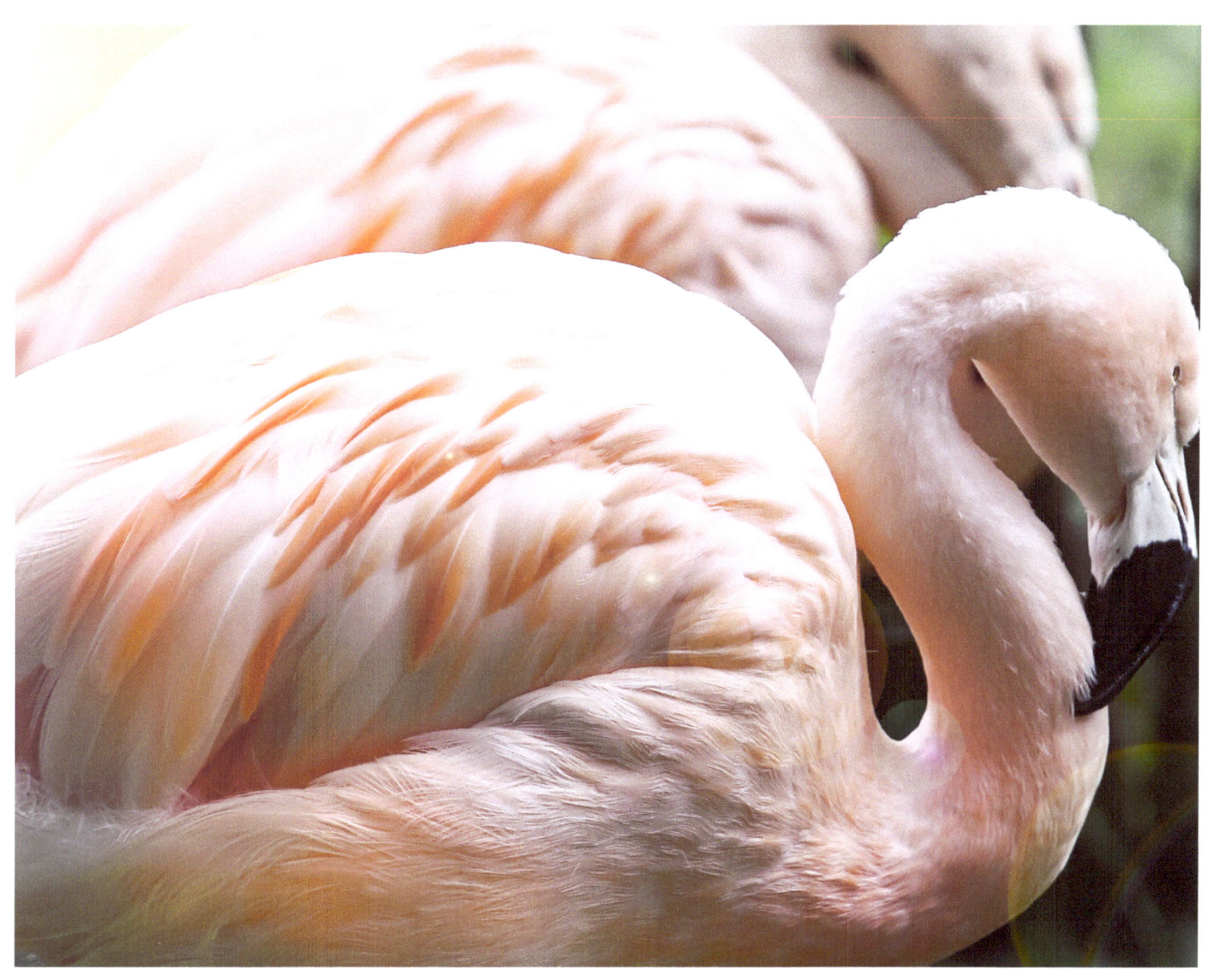

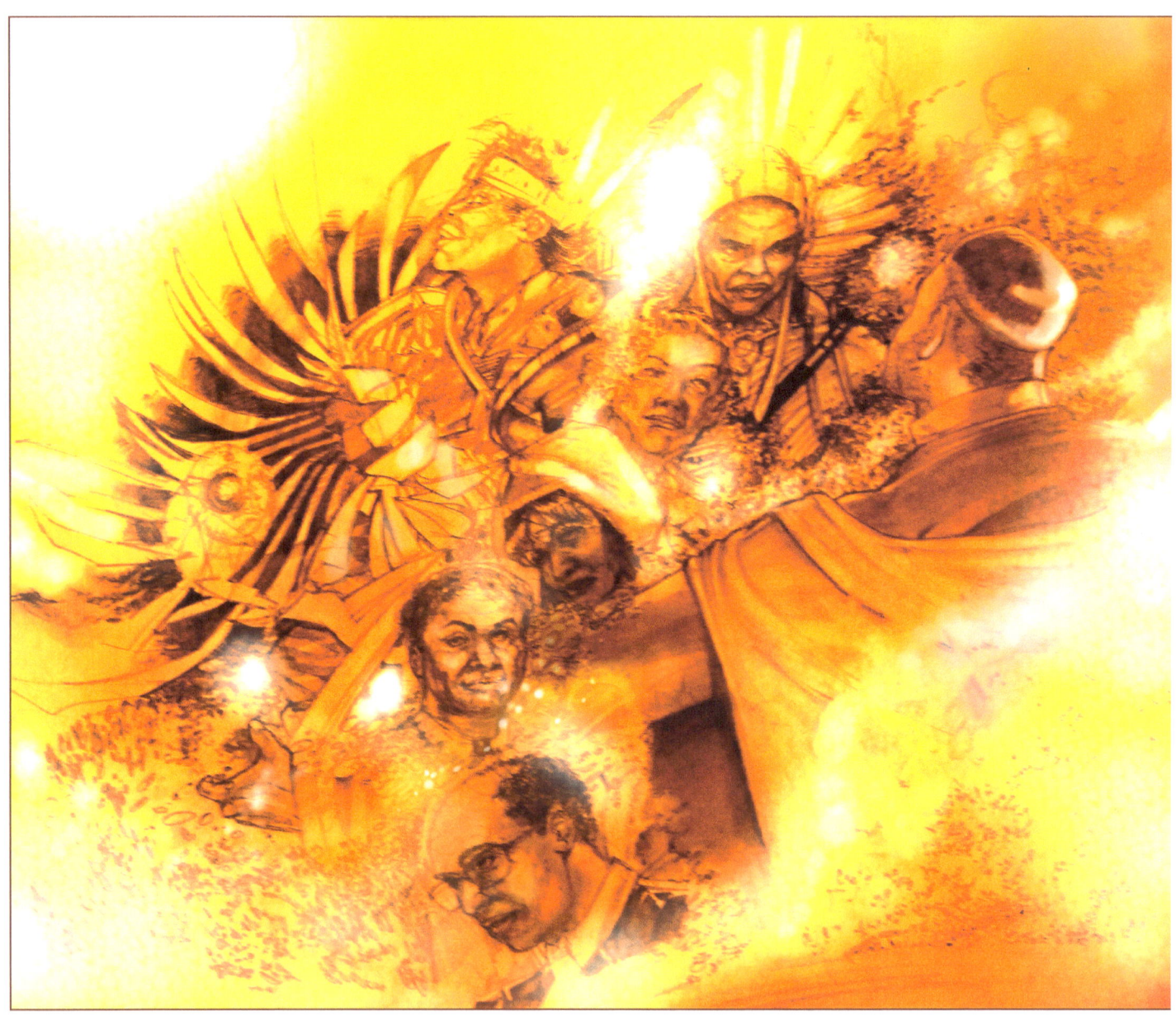

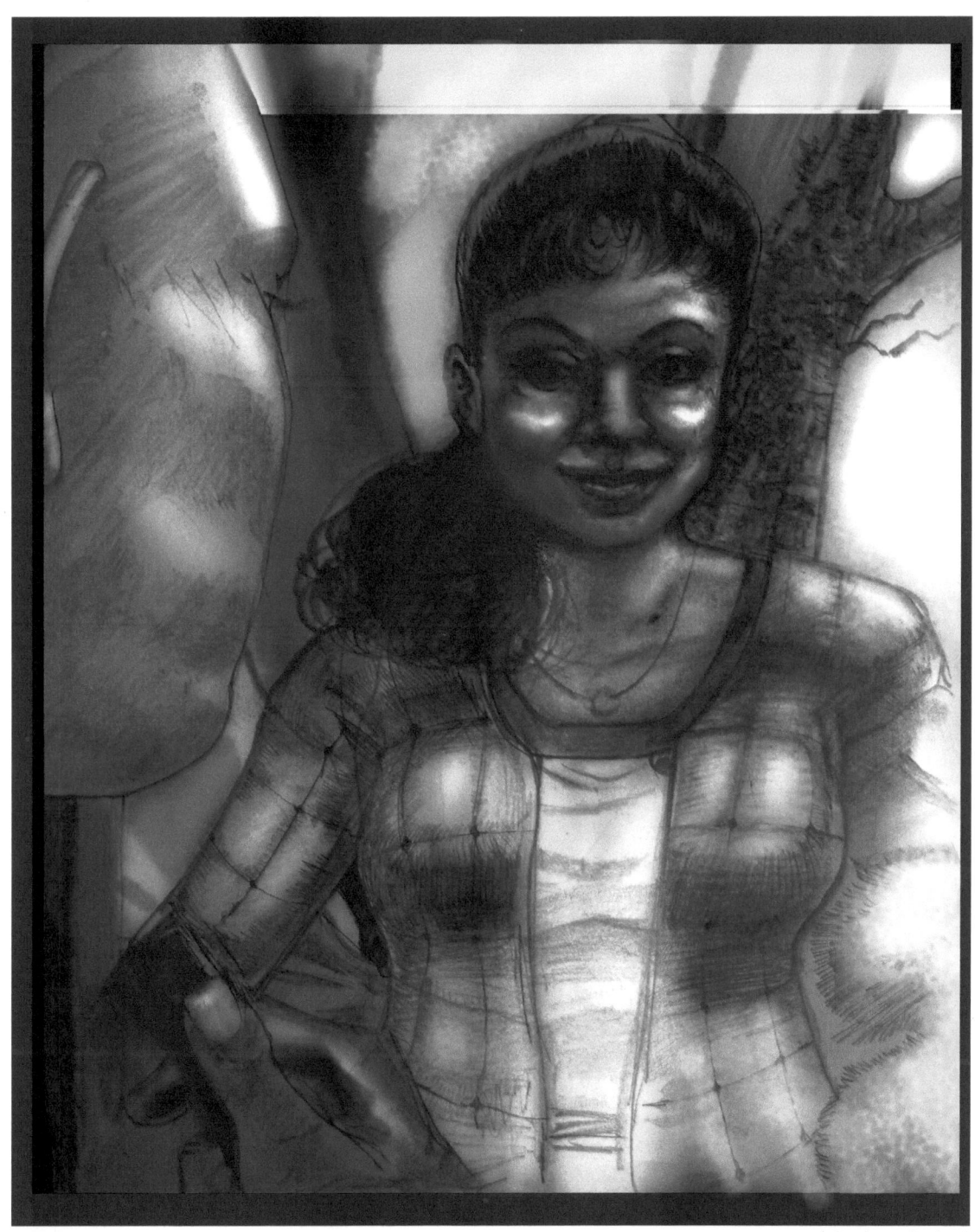

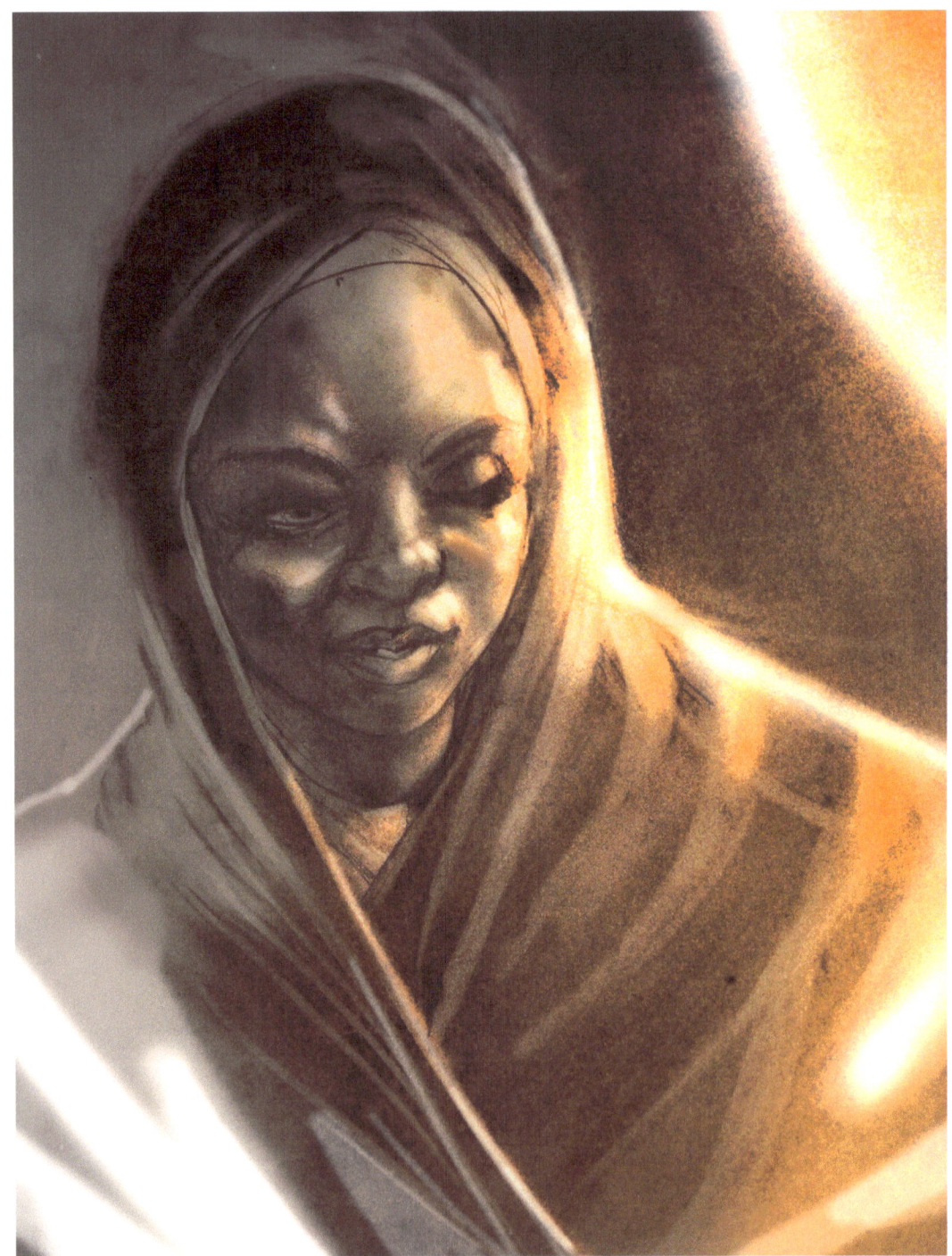
richardson, herbert

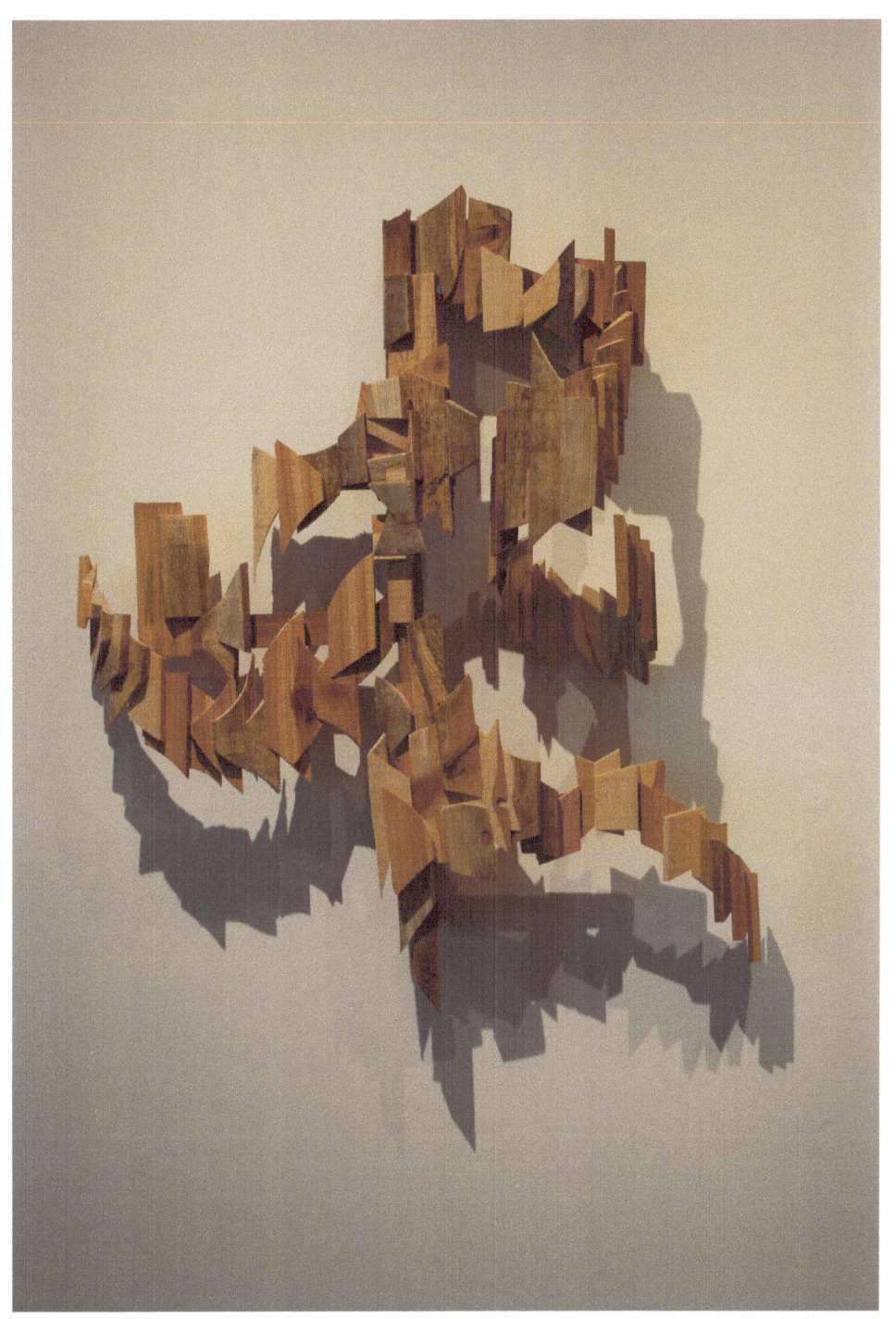

godden, anna

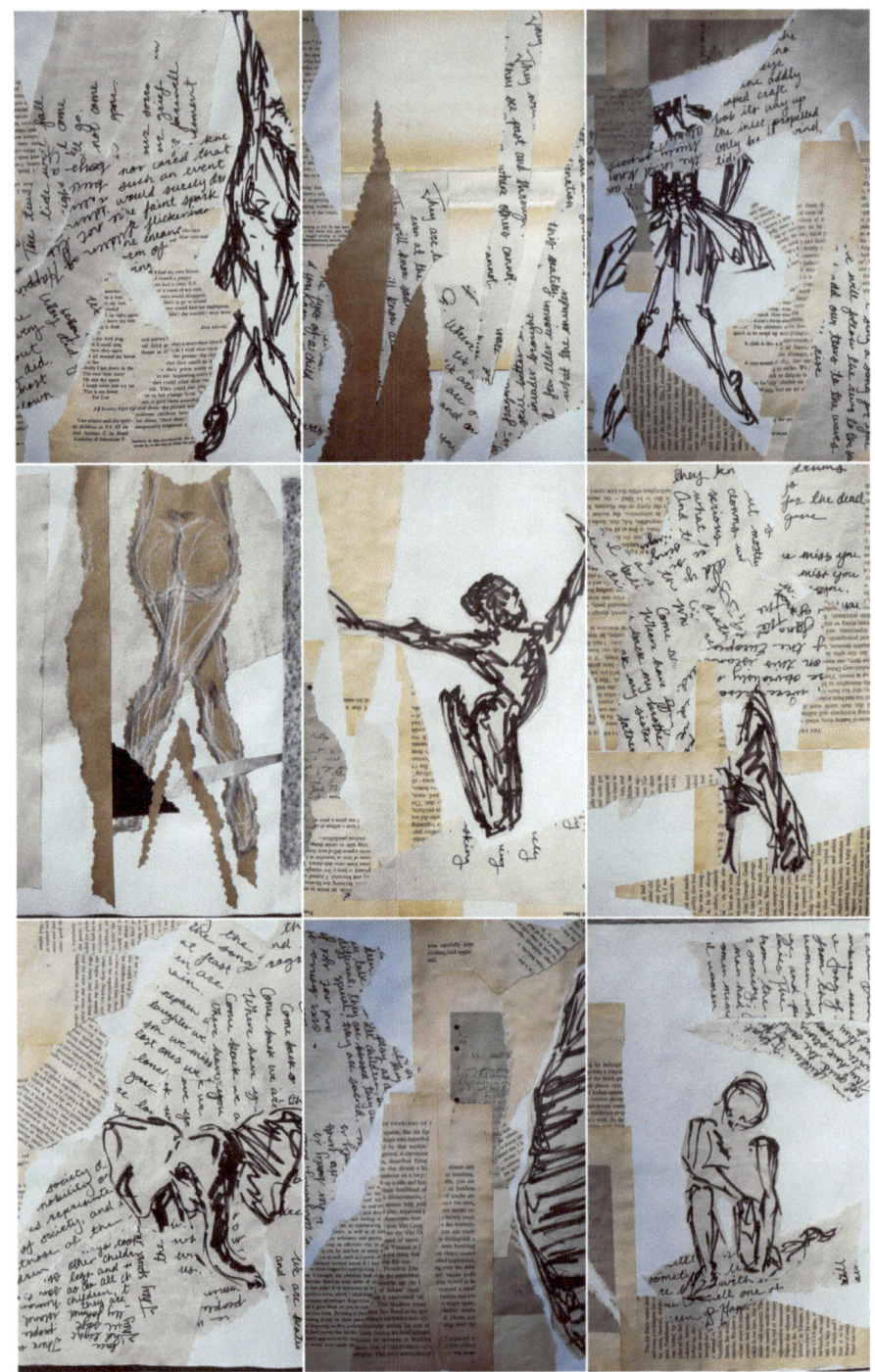

godden, anna

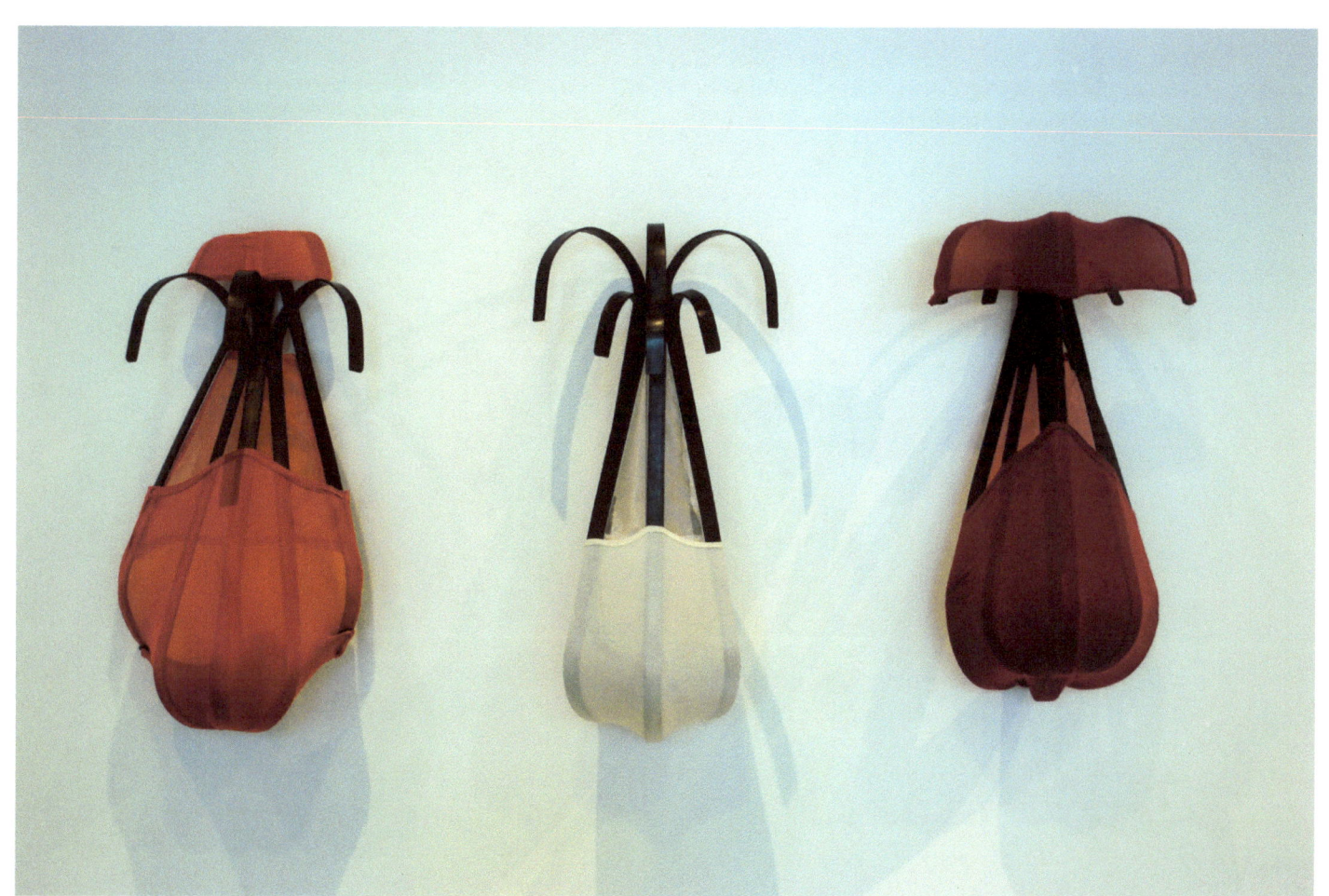

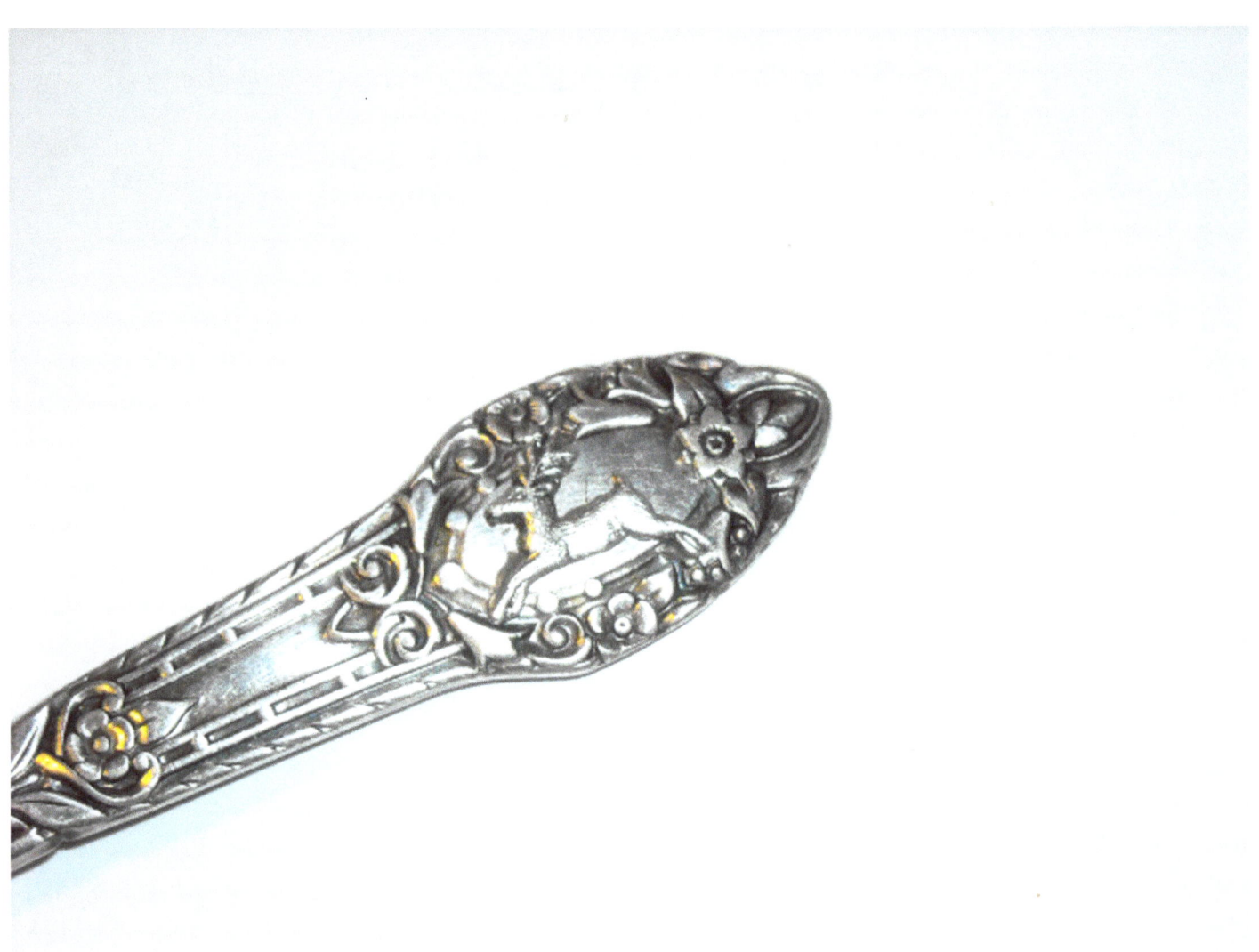

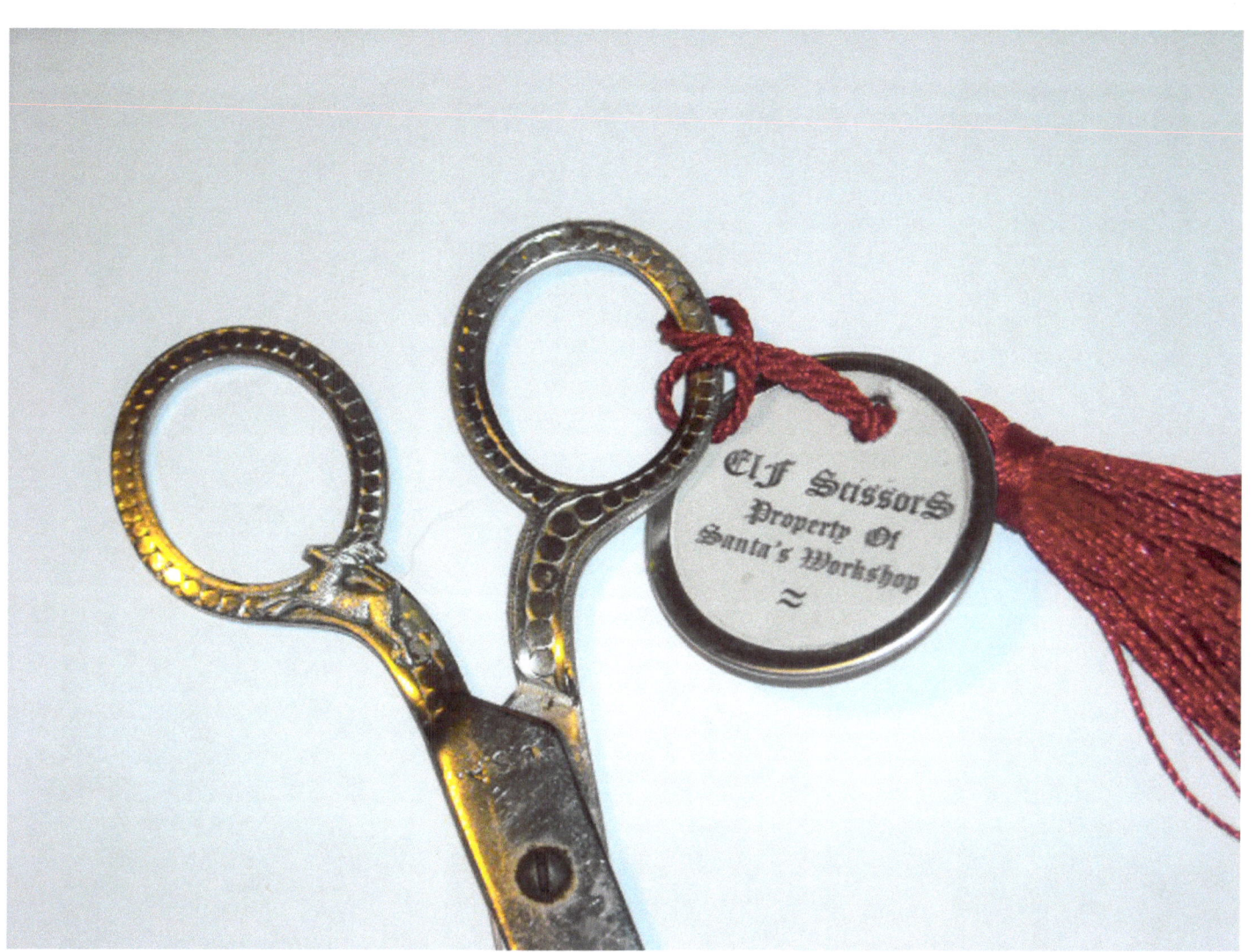

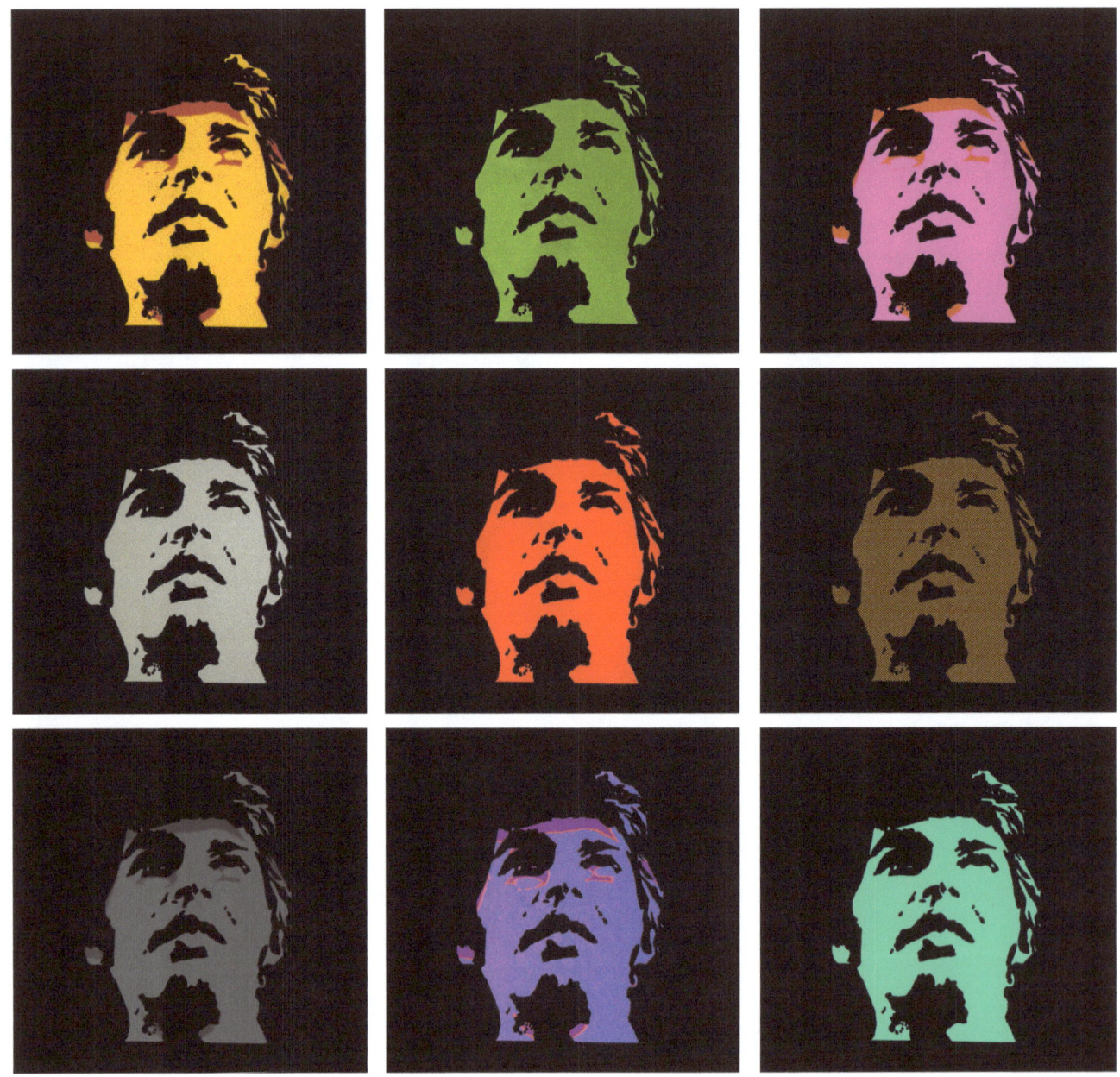

rivera, graciela

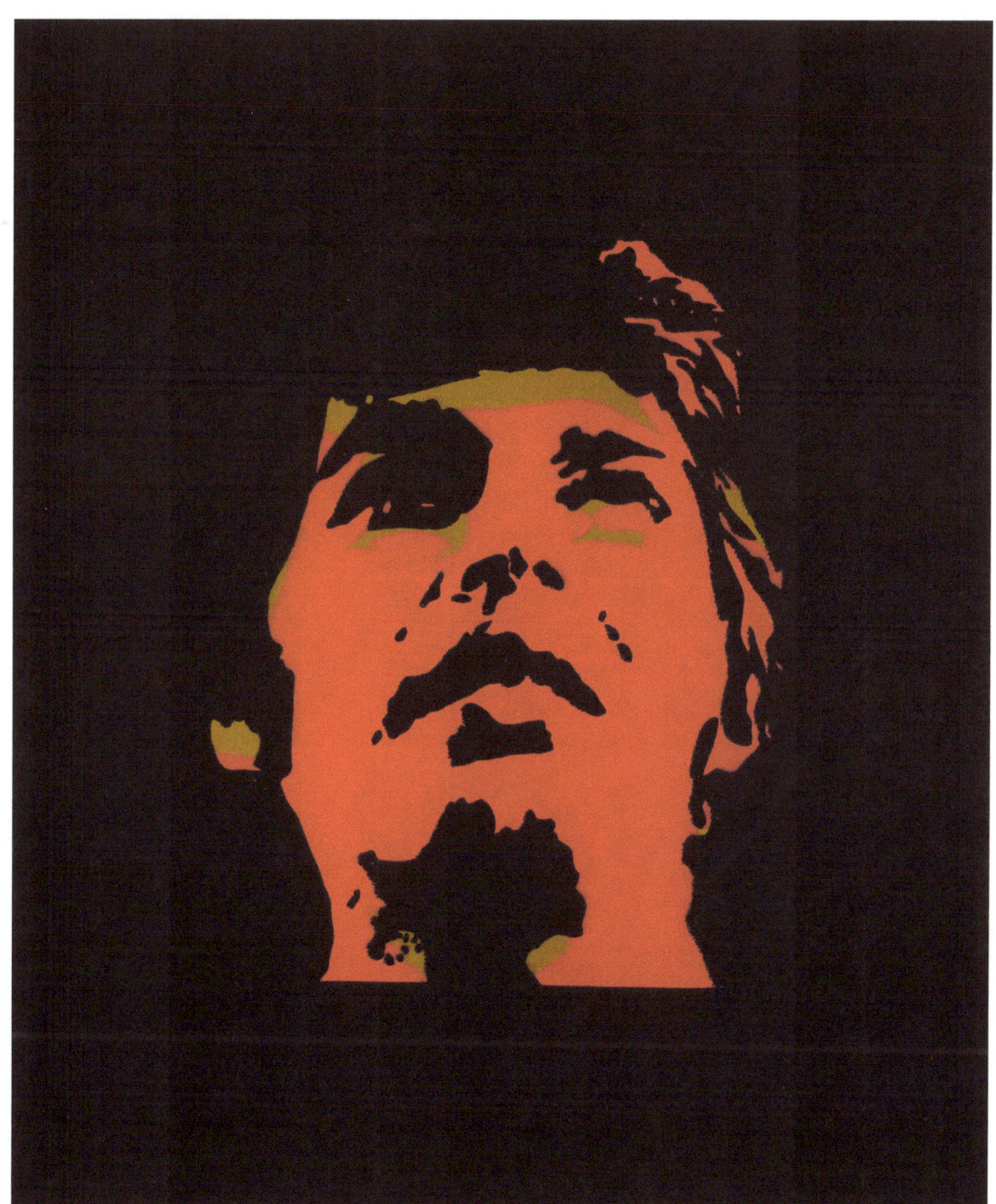

rivera, graciela

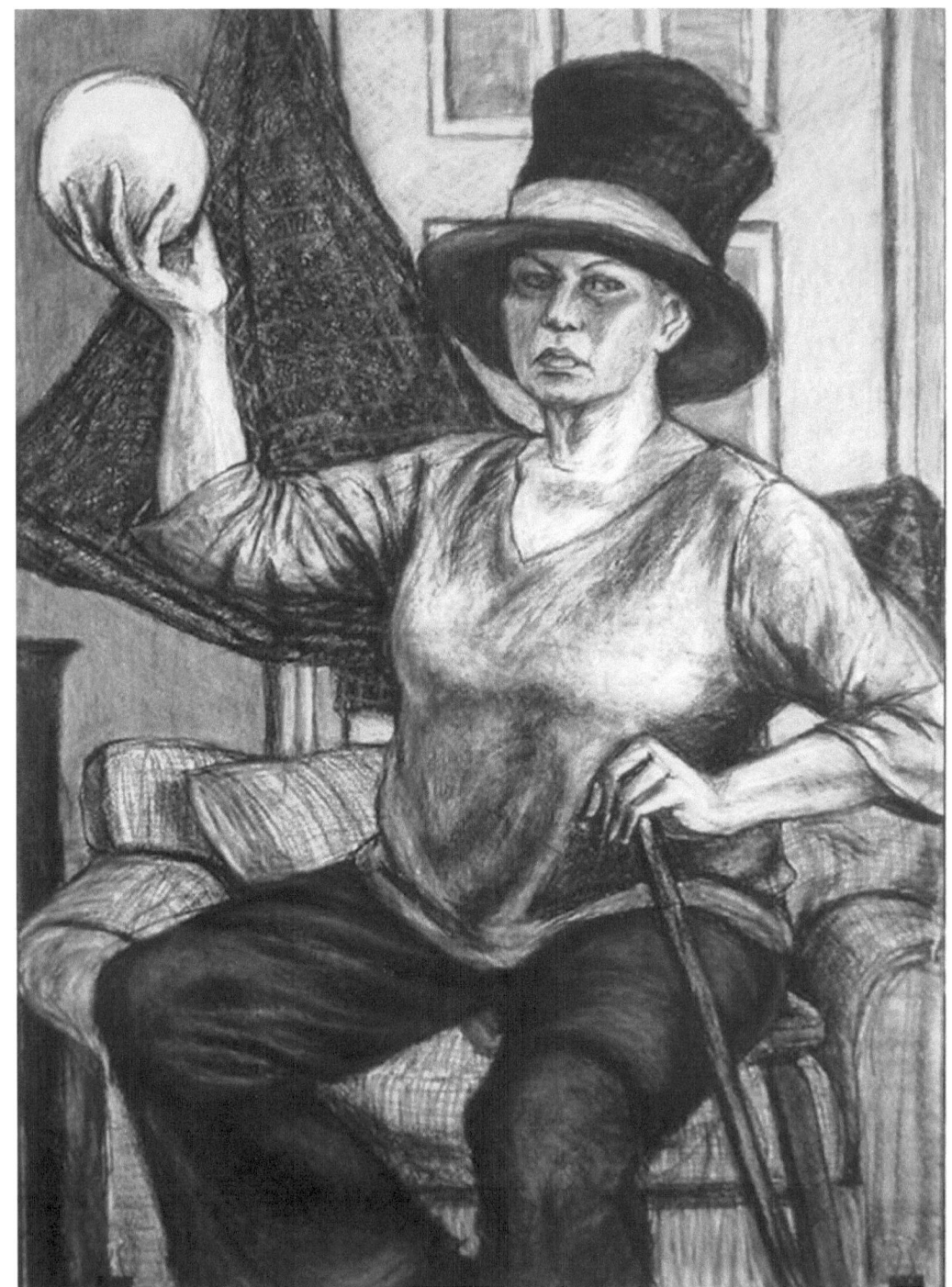

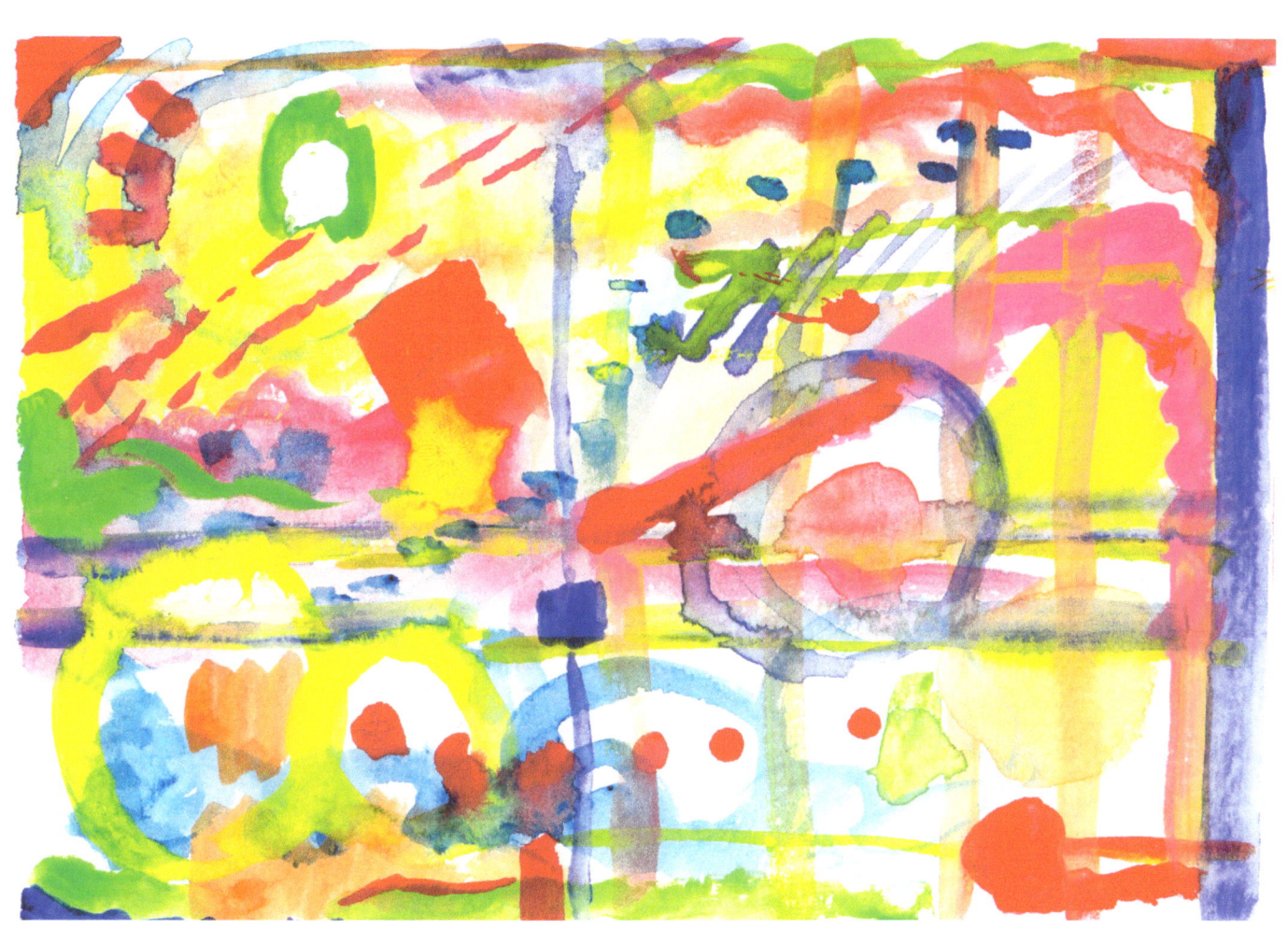

barr, m g

the eyes that feel,

ananian, michael
  hocus pocus!..................8
    casein on paper, 26.5" x 22"
  sesame!.....................9
    casein on paper, 26.5" x 22"
  abracadabra!................10
    casein on paper, 26.5" x 22"
  tadah!......................11
    casein on paper, 26.5" x 22"
  presto!.....................12
    casein on paper, 26.5" x 22"

barr, m g (marilynn g)
  ichiban vase................3
    oil on canvas, 24" x 24"
  shipwrecked.................13
    pastels on paper, 19" x 25"
  lights in the attic........38
    pastels on paper, 38" x 49"
  woman i, woman you, women we...............39
    digital collage, graphite on paper, 15" x 16"
  golden sword................57
    pastels on paper, 19" x 25"
  mad hatter..................78
    charcoal on paper, 32" x 48"
  water coloring at SASA......79
    watercolor, 7" x 5"

barr, j a
  reflections.................14
    colored pencil on paper, 11" x 14"
  pins n needles..............14, 15
    straight pins and foam core sculpture
    9.5" x 9.5" x 2.5"
  head........................16
    ink on paper, 16" x 20"

belluardo, s a
  stalking the moon...........56
    photographs, digital collage, 12" x 12"

campbell-thomas, barbara
  green/grey jump.............4
    acrylic, ink, & collage on paper, 8.5" x 11"
  yellow/pink (pieces)........5
    acrylic, ink, & collage on paper, 8.5" x 11"
  pierced orange loop.........6
    acrylic, ink, & collage on paper, 8.5" x 11"
  pink and orange triangle....7
    acrylic, ink, & collage on paper, 8.5" x 11"

foust, s
  reindeer fork...............74
    photograph, 7.5" x 5.5"
  reindeer scissors...........75
    photograph, 7.5" x 5.5"

godden, anna
  transitions.................71
    wood, 3' x 3'
  9 minutes...................72
    collage, 9 pieces, each 9" x 11"
  suspended figures...........73
    steel and cloth, 3 pieces
    2.5' x 1' x 1'

mckenzie, alex
  studio view of geoboard.....17
    wood, nails, rubber bands, 8' x 8'
  rbs (compilation 12/1000)...18
    mixed media on paper, 5" x 5" each
  efs (compilation 20/100)....19
    intaglio, 7.5" x 7.5" each
  untitled....................20
    oil on canvas, 30" x 50"
  untitled....................21
    oil on canvas, 48" x 60"

moore, maurice
  visible.....................40
    collage mixed media, 36" x 44"-8.5" x 11"
  more adventurous............40
    charcoal on paper, 75' x 5'
  visible.....................41
    collage mixed media, 36" x 44"-8.5" x 11"
  more adventurous............41
    charcoal on paper, 75' x 5'
  fairy.......................42
    charcoal on paper, 4' x 7'

morris, christopher h
  untitled (cloudscape 3).....22
    oil on canvas, 53" x 46"
  silver lining...............23
    charcoal on paper, 18" x 24"
  before the storm............24
    charcoal and graphite on mylar, 18" x 24"
  untitled (cloudscape 4).....25
    oil on canvas, 72" x 65"

note: dimensions are listed width by height

the hands that see

neff, j
- sarah.. 63
  - photograph, 14" x 11"
- ave.. 64
  - photograph, 11" x 14"
- sky.. 65
  - photograph, 14" x 10.5"
- family... 66
  - photograph, 14" x 11"
- flamingos.. 67
  - photograph, 14" x 11"

pintado, steisha
- landscape.. 26
  - oil on paper monotype, 8" x 10"
- self-portrait, see through............................. 27
  - oil on paper monotype, 10" x 8"
- self-portrait, solid strong............................ 28
  - oil on paper monotype, 10" x 8"
- energize... 29
  - oil on canvas, 48" x 36"

richardson, herbert
- embers of saponi....................................... 68
  - watercolor, graphite, chalk on paper, 14" x 11"
- portraits working...................................... 69
  - graphite on paper, 8.5" x 11"
- sagittarius by lamplight............................... 70
  - graphite, copic markers on paper, 8.5" x 11"

rivera, graciela
- sandro * 9... 76
  - digital collage, 12" x 12"
- sandro... 77
  - silk screen on paper, 16" x 20"

robinson, miranda
- what's the buzz.. 47
  - photograph, 12" x 9"
- jocelyn.. 48
  - photograph, 12" x 9"
- bud.. 49
  - photograph, 9" x 12"

said, ibrahim
- black stacked circles.................................. 30
  - white earthenware, 11.75" x 12"
- black double circles................................... 31
  - porcelain, 10" x 10"
- vase with handles...................................... 32
  - porcelain, 8.5" x 18"
- double cone jug-filter................................. 33
  - red earthenware, 6.5" x 7.5"

shipman, bennett
- nudes in motion.. 50
  - charcoal, 18" x 20"
- blender.. 51
  - oil on canvas, 16" x 20"
- self-portrait.. 52
  - oil on canvas, 18" x 24"
- portals.. 53
  - oil on convas, 18" x 24"
- circle portrait.. 54
  - charcoal, 24" x 24"
- circle still life..................................... 55
  - oil on canvas, 24" x 24"

stephan, mariam
- rock slide... 34
  - oil on stretched canvas, 50" x 68"
- nest box... 35
  - oil on cut canvas, 68" x 53"
- foundation touch....................................... 36
  - oil on stretched canvas, 72" x 56"
- yellow frame... 37
  - oil on canvas, 70" x 64"

swift, nicholas
- felix and amelia frames................................ 58
  - animation stills
- rider in the mist..................................... 59
  - digital illustration
- girl on dragon.. 60
  - animation stills
- model sheet-kai....................................... 61
  - graphite digital illustration
- like a dream.. 62
  - digital illustration

tisdell, suzanne
- pandora... 43
  - charcoal on paper, 22" x 30"
- callisto.. 44
  - charcoal on paper, 22" x 30"
- he knew what came next................................ 45
  - charcoal on paper, 22" x 30"
- daphne.. 46
  - charcoal on paper, 22" x 30"

to contact "the eyes that feel, the hands that see" featured in the starving artist, please write to:

the starving artist
little acorn associates, inc.
post office box 8787
greensboro, nc 27419-0787

sasa™

the starving artist
eyes that feel, hands that see
is an annual by-invitation publication

to be considered for inclusion,
please write to:

SASA
Post Office Box 8787
Greensboro, North Carolina 27419-0787

www.ingramcontent.com/pod-product-compliance
Lightning Source LLC
Chambersburg PA
CBHW051156220526
45473CB00003B/798